Melody and Silence

the selfish bodhisattva

Melody and Silence

the selfish bodhisattva

Chobo

BOOKS

Winchester, UK
Washington, USA

First published by O-Books, 2012
O-Books is an imprint of John Hunt Publishing Ltd., Laurel House, Station Approach,
Alresford, Hants, SO24 9JH, UK
office1@jhpbooks.net
www.johnhuntpublishing.com

For distributor details and how to order please visit the 'Ordering' section on our website.

Text copyright: Chobo 2011

ISBN: 978 1 78099 547 2

A CIP catalogue record for this book is available from the British Library.

Design: Stuart Davies

Printed and bound by CPI Group (UK) Ltd, Croydon, CR0 4YY

We operate a distinctive and ethical publishing philosophy in all
areas of our business, from our global network of authors to
production and worldwide distribution.

CONTENTS

Acknowledgments

There are so many friends who have danced with me on this indescribable journey of life. You know who you are. I would like to mention a couple though, without whom this book would not be.

My loving partner Jennifer for her editorial help and unquestioning support. Words cannot express my gratitude, only tears.

It is said, as one traverses the path of being it becomes narrower and narrower, until one is all alone, and then with all the world. I would like to express my love to three of my friends who travelled with me, for so long. I am privileged to have known such genuine truth seekers. Christopher Higgo, Yoga master; Allen Crosson, master of the Eastern arts: ninjitsu and acupuncture; and Niraja, master of nothing.

The beloved Mevlana Mooji, who cut off my head and set me free.

This book has a special dedication for Paul Bourke. May you see you are already That, in which you are striving to be.

You are love.
The one that has love, loses love. The one that wants love and idealizes love is the ego, hence all love affairs are coming and going through a personality. At some point one has to disappear as a person in order to be a being and that being is love and, as Ramana said, all good qualities arise naturally from this. One neither likes nor dislikes because one is content and full of love already. Your own being is more than you could possibly hope for.

Forgetting the Self is like forgetting what sunshine is. Even though it is sunny every day, we suffer because we want sunshine. We may even search and read books describing what sunshine is, all in the presence of sunshine itself. One day we meet a master who says, 'It is already sunny, you managed to find your way here by the light of the sun.' You have an insight! Then the doubt comes back; could it be that simple? Then you drop all ideas and simply see the blinding, obvious truth of it. And when you do, it is so simple and obvious it is truly laughable. And like a solved puzzle, you can't believe no one else can see how obvious it is.

Spiritual disclaimers

I would like to make a few points clear before we begin. (Interestingly, every chapter of this book was the beginning at some point – there are no beginnings, not for me. That is the first point.)

Secondly, I have no interest in spirituality at all. None. For me, there is only life, and nothing can be separated from life, therefore everything is contained within life. Higher and lower, or I am better than you – or my concepts of life are better than your concepts – are all the same in that they are all part of life. You may agree, disagree, like or dislike but all the differences are the same. This is a book about life. What is. It is nothing to do with categorizations. It is about clearing out all ideas of yourself; looking at yourself freshly, without any thought of gain or loss. Just who you are. As will be restated – is who you are spiritual? Or do you exist before the concept of spirituality? Do you need to know the right words to know who you are or can you find out your own truth without a dogma?

I am a human being, are you? That means I have multidimensional aspects. I can dream, fart, love, play, conceptualize, point out something via negativa or via positiva, joke, be intense, be silent, be loud, share ideas and drop ideas. If we are trying to be spiritual or religious we will be burdened by the concepts we have of them. We will have subtle or not so subtle restraints and tensions due to how we feel a 'spiritual' person is.

Third, I know nothing.

Chobo: How are you?

A: I had a bit of a panic attack today, but I think I'm okay again now. My head is broken, maybe you could tell me again what you told me last week?

C: I am very happy your head is broken.

Everything that is happening to you is happening in the realm of your consciousness, or beingness, or perception. You are aware of your panic attack. This means you are beyond the emotional wave of a panic attack. It comes and goes within your being. Stay with the sense of being that does not come and go. Remember – it is not an object, it is an intuitive sense: 'I am.' Every living being has a natural intuitive sense of existing. It requires no effort to exist, for your being to be here and know life is happening.

Stay with this sense, feel that nothing can be added to your being, this sense of self. Thoughts come and go and are merely observed, they are not fought, do not wish them away, just be aware that you are aware of them so they cannot be who you are. You remain; they come and go. You cannot be that which comes and goes. You are the one aware of coming and going. You are here, this sense of being is always here; is there any suffering? Pain may come and go, but watch what happens if you simply stay an observer; do you suffer? A panic attack comes, stay as the witness, just be aware that you are the one in which panic attacks are happening. Now ask the question – who is the one that is aware, what is this self that is aware, that is formless, that simply is, can it be found?

If you are really having trouble specifically with panic attacks then use this as your main tool for enquiry. Who is having the panic attack? Who is the one suffering from it, is this one real? Is this one not also perceived? Does this one not also come and go? Watch all the thoughts that trigger the emotions of a panic attack. They are just thoughts, but when one grabs them, when they are believed in they become feelings and cripple us, but the same thoughts may not trouble someone else at all. This shows the thought has no power of its own; you are giving it the power, watch this. If you can dis-identify with the thoughts, this is true freedom. Watch them arise as objects, separate from your sense of being. Perceived by you, yes, but not you. If you are compelled by them, by habit, notice that this too is observed. If you feel like it, sit for 10 minutes just being naturally aware of your sense of being and how it is always as it is. Don't try and find peace by getting rid of anything but find it in the midst of emotional storms.

Don't be intellectual; this witnessing is how to be the master of your own self, it is a very direct approach, no words are needed, no spirituality, no religion, just you staying as your being a light unto yourself. Don't seek any state other than life as it is here now.

A: Wow. I just closed my eyes for a bit and felt the energy I'm aware of without giving it any name. It's amazing. And it's the very same stuff that I could call nerves, or fear, or by any name. Except it's actually so vibrant and vast.

C: Yes. And it is within you, there is no imagination involved, no need to try to reach to some idea of how it should be, no image. One starts to see. This seeing is fathomless. You may start to notice that all your energies that happen within you are quite natural and – without thinking they are good or bad – come and flow quite naturally and spontaneously, all watched with an undercurrent of peace, spaciousness. This inner gratitude that the divine is who you are is true prayer without words. As much as possible just keep quiet. Don't name it, say it out loud, but gently feel everywhere you go that, no matter what happens, your being just stays the same.

I want you to be free

Freedom from can be very subtle. If we wish to attain enlightenment, this is freedom from. But if the wish to find freedom never arises, one will never be free. The wish takes us so far, it takes us to the path. So freedom from is important. If we are carrying a heavy load it can be helpful to put it down for a moment to regain our breath. Sometimes it is helpful to run away to get a modicum of space to realign so that we can have a better chance to find the real. Freedom comes when we drop the wish to even be free. We accept at a 'being' level everything that happens to us, such as, if you are saying to yourself 'trust life and accept' you are not because you are still hoping, however subtle, for a better outcome by accepting. Part of true acceptance is accepting where we truly are even if it hurts the ego to admit we are still as 'ordinary' in our jealousies, annoyances, avoidances, as anyone else. In this humility of nothingness, magic happens.

There is no place to start. The truth has been written about thousands of times and still is has never been said. Each expression, however, is a flower of beauty too. We are multidimensional beings and the capacities of life are fathomless. We have to give ourselves the freedom to express and explore life in all its dimensions. At the heart of life, the deepest core of being is awareness. Awareness beyond body and mind. However, the mind too is beautiful; the body is beautiful. Although the deepest truths cannot be said, the beauty of a free being expressing themselves with the mind is also a beauty. Using the mind is helpful in order to overcome the mind. It is not that difficult to understand. We neither cling to an idea that the mind is useless nor cling to any words said. The truth is inexhaustible in its expressions. If we are open to beauty, life in all its dimensions, each expression has a joy of its own. There are not many more things on this earth more beautiful than a Buddha's mind. His words, his expression of a state beyond words, beyond mind. What a mysterious and utterly beautiful world. The truth is forever deepening, elusive. They say a game of chess has infinite variation; you will never play two games the same. A game of chess – what to say about life!

We may, however, suffer from boredom! Life is not boring, but by some bizarre twist of fate we have become identified with the mind. The mechanism for labeling. We have substituted the mysterious infinity and endless variation of experiencing for words in our head. We think we know what a tree is because we have been taught what the word tree is. Or we have acquired other data through the mind about a tree. We may have another sound banging between our ears for the tree such as 'oak.' This sound may again give us a deeper deception that we know what a tree is, or we may know the time it takes to grow or any other outside data. However, these are mere sounds in our head. We do not know what a tree is. This process of labeling and defining and thinking we know life through the words we have gathered is what makes us bored, and hence fired up with desire. This process of defining and living through the mind and being attached to our identification with what the mind says is the block to all the glories of life. Life is right here, it is *us*! We are the infinite mystery. Everyone and everything we meet is unknowable mystery. If we are moving through life with this as the overriding inner self then we can use the mind to increase the wonder and not bind us. If someone says to us, 'There is a crow,' we do not think, 'Oh yes, I know what a crow is.' It is more like, 'Crow! That is the label for that unknowable expression of life moving through the sky, what is it? What is black? How can such a life exist? How can such a thing be?!' That is more the flavor, unspoken, simply marveling at this astonishing creature that exists and can be perceived! It is life. What is the meaning of life? Your life is the meaning of life.

The meaning of life is living it. Life is not something outside of you but it can appear that way if you are living through your labels. The labels are deep rooted; they have been pounded into us from birth. Absolutely necessary and needed but we need to transcend their influence. We don't destroy ourselves, our mind, our body, we simply recognize it is something we move beyond. Obviously in and of themselves learning the names for objects and attaining knowledge is not what a Buddha is. One of the difficulties in attaining or remembering our true nature or inner Buddha or awakening is that deep and constant association with words also produces feelings that go with them, hence giving us a deep sense we think we know something through knowledge.

Even though we are not living in contented bliss, we still cling to our identity because it seems that is where we have ever found even the smallest bit of happiness. In actual fact, it is all we know. Our identification with mind is pervasive. This being said we know there is a deeper space. We say things like, 'There must be more to life.' The meaning of life is thus found outside the mind's idea of meaning.

The mind is cunning. This book arose in response to the endless capabilities mind has of holding on to identity, tripping itself up with logic and the inherent pride that goes with it which stinks up the pure and open being.

The mind has a built-in fundamentalist attitude. Whatever 'it' is involved in is the best. Whatever 'it' is doing is the right thing. It always feels right and both strongly and subtly condemns other paths and people. It finds it unbearable that someone else may have it right and it isn't getting it. It wants to make everything a thing, in which it fits into place. Wants to make distinctions such as Sufism or Advaita in order to feel higher than others. It can even become fundamentalist about the teachings of no self, the teachings of oneness, as if the teachings of another religion are separate from that oneness, or the oneness has lower levels to it. Thus, hidden in their language, is the sense that they are still the same as before they realized this 'oneness' – except they have a super spiritual, non-spiritual identity.

We sense it; we sense both traps. That the inner Self, the inner God, the inner Buddha, the being within beyond words and free from suffering is not something outside ourselves that we have to work and work and work on. We 'have to' follow the self-sustaining traditions, so they can be maintained, so that all the time spent in it actually pays off because you get to control and tell others what to do eventually. That through it all we will finally be someone in the eyes of others, a deep secret self will finally be recognized and it will be pointed out by the super beings who we have been following because then it will have extra special super meaning. We sense it is not that, it is not a constant carrot before the donkey.

We also sense it is not the cheap weekend enlightenment. People claiming to be enlightened, who still get just as angry, just as often, just as jealous, just as annoyed as they ever were, but say they are a witness. They say you don't need to do anything ever and laugh arrogantly at those who have a practice. Who break through one layer of conditioning and claim they've got it. Who have a nice smile, and their intellectual understanding gives them lovely feelings and they are conveniently in the moment and following their hearts when it suits them. We sense this is not it.

We are pure, whole, beyond measure. This is in no way a lofty statement of measurement against others but only against the limited identity you are holding on to. You are the same consciousness as any Buddha. It is not something far away nor is it accessed and lived just by understanding intellectually. It is, however, easily findable. It is you, yes! You. It is not an idea, it is not a thought, it is consciousness. It is your birthright. The adventure of adventure is discovering your own being again. It is the awareness before any information was given to it. You are always consciousness, the idea of who you are comes and goes every day in different shapes and sizes. Even a change of coat

7

can be a change of identity. All these changes happen to the one who never changes. We know this. We know there is a one who has never changed. Who is this one? The one in whom information was given, in whom ideas arise of how one can attain to that state? Who are you?

I want to take you on a journey of mystery and adventure. The ideas that follow may vary and fluctuate from via positiva to via negativa. After decades of seeking, I had the funny realization one day that I had no philosophy, no teaching, no belief, had nothing to comment on – nothing to put forward. I had the fortune of finding true masters. For me, this is the true sense of the usage of words to break all other word structures, patterns and beliefs. As can be seen and, as I am using words, this does not mean they need to be abandoned. That is too extreme. We may abandon them for a while – there are no rules to life. If you are holding on to ideas, you have missed. The ideas I am using here are for your personal entertainment and recognition. Some of you may delight in them; that delight is personal and that delight can lead to the end of the person. If the person is finished then you will meet people spontaneously without an agenda, open, ready to explore. If so, the words were a beautiful sharing of two people together on this mysterious spaceship traveling through the universe.

I want you to be free. Free to feel what is right, free to be disciplined or free to have no practice. Ideas can help. Ideas can hinder. We live in a world of ideas and language. It is the 99%. Mind. The idea that ideas can be dropped is different from other ideas that if followed, looked into, will help end ideas. If it is held on to as a belief and doesn't ignite an existential lived experience of truth, it will hinder. Simple.

So be wary of people who say not to follow any ideas and do not do any practice, for that is an idea too and they are therefore teaching. Something extreme. And be wary of those who build spiritual empires on ideas and use the stimulation to propel themselves and their prestige.

If we are an open seeker, we can see many rotten institutions. But we are small and individual, and they may have millions of followers, and clever argumentation and great scholars. To stand up against them can be daunting. Our small intuitive sense of a natural, simple, joyous, spontaneous life can be trampled on.

Take it as a great challenge to follow your own truth *and* remain open, free flowing. Not condemning anyone; allowing others their freedom. Freedom is a strange thing because it allows others to be free to try and destroy the freedom itself and try to impose their dogmas.

I want to be a friendly voice in the vast expanse of life who says:

'The intuitive feeling you have that spirituality is not even spirituality. It is being natural, alive, creative, joyful, playful, mysterious, a great, great laughter deep with one's own meditation, one's simple awareness, one's own light...'

... is right. It has nothing to do with following someone, although following someone is almost always necessary. It is has nothing to do with a spiritual community, although finding a spirit-minded family is beautiful. It is finding your own true self, which is already here, and it is the same self as all selves have ever been and will be. You are only a thought away from freedom. In the end, only you can free yourself. Although we may be drenched in our identities: martial artist, workshop leader, poet, Tantric teacher, golfer, perfect disciple, world-renowned artist, they are all something we have believed in over time. They have arrived in our consciousness and they will just as easily disappear when we die. Our chance is to drop all ideas, beliefs and identities that have arisen before our true self and find the great bottomless mystery within. If, on your journey, you have belonged to a dogmatic creed in the past such as

Christianity or Buddhism – great – acknowledge the pains and joys, but ask, 'Has it truly brought me to freedom?' If not, what is more important – my ideas to find freedom or freedom itself? Only you can answer it. When the great master Papaji arrived at Ramana's door, he told him his life thus far had led him to where he is now. No need to cling to it or dislike it. It served its purpose. We may have needed a new catalogue of dogmas to believe in because our old ones were so painful, but the truth lies beyond all dogmas – it lies beyond the mind. Consciousness is the source of truth. Ideas coming from truth are not the truth. There is a time to drop the path that is simply swapping ideas for the one where ideas have to be dropped. It has to happen. Are you before the mind and its ideas or was your being summoned into existence by the mind? If your being is before the mind, then this is where the truth lies.

A: I feel lonely; doesn't that mean something's cutting me off from myself? But how can it, in reality? 'Loneliness' is such a pest! Do you never feel it?

Chobo: I don't know if it has any meaning or needs to be figured out with the mind. That's the first place to start: 'I feel lonely. I don't want to experience anything else, because if I impose anything, I am again falling into the same trap of imposing my ideas on life.' If loneliness means anything it will be contained in the experience of being lonely. Once you don't want to not be lonely, gently look within and see who is lonely. I am never lonely. I never miss anyone and I am never bored. My being is such joy. So is yours; for some reason the mere thought that you need something else prevents! It's a mysterious existence.

And if I can find this, my god, anyone can!

A: Didn't you have to meditate on love for years?

C: Yet, I've always been this. How weird and mysterious can it possibly be! Just a thought away... but a thought believed in has such gravity.

Life not dogma

Life is our religion, all beings our sangha, living life our sadhana, and our goal is happening right now.

My gentle and continuous reminder is: It is simple, clear and obvious.

We somehow intuitively know the truth very easily. Why? Because we *are* the truth. We are the deep experience we have been seeking outside ourselves for! What a mysterious world. The truth is as deep as we are within ourselves. The tendency of the mind is to calculate and quantify everything. This is perfection when working out how to build a house that won't collapse on our heads. It is misplaced usage, and the result of an incorrect understanding and education when it tries to quantify and pigeonhole consciousness.

It is simple to understand. If I tell you there is a ball in the room; one person sees it as red, the other person sees it as blue. What color is it? Even if we try to say one person is color-blind we still have to define the true color through the person and what we consider to be a defect.

There is some food on the table. One person receives bliss and joy by eating it, the other is sick after eating it. Is it good food or bad?

A band is playing. One person likes the music, the other person does not. Are they a good band or not? In fact, if the one person is outnumbered a million to one, can we ever say the band is good?

It is simple, clear and obvious that our experience of the world depends on us. In our current world, this inner being is forgotten about. We develop refined culture around the mind's opinions, we can obtain degrees and doctorates and analyze the entire universe, but if we have forgotten the simple truth that the world is dependent on the perceiver, that life is a subjective experience, we will never be at peace.

We know this. We, in general, ignore it. We are still allured by the outer world and the projections of ego; mainly because society is the collective need to live together and that need requires outer fulfillment. We can never have an enlightened society because society is what we see through in order to attain truth. Truth is finding your inner witness; it is an individual, subjective knowing. We need to eat, sleep, find shelter and take care of all the human needs our body requires. We have done this amazingly well, to the point where we can travel to the other side of the world in less than a day by flying through the sky. Not only can we fly but we can have a cup of tea while doing so. We can talk to any friend almost anywhere in the world; we can even see them on the other side of the world. We can think of a song and within seconds we can find it and play it in our room. We have the choice of foods from anywhere on the planet. We live in a world of miracles. To have reached this stage, we have progressed from the need to survive out of fear of animals, and finding shelter, and having to strive to get there. If humans were just sitting around doing nothing we wouldn't have progressed to where we are now. Through our work and breakthroughs we finally attained a stage where fears, hard work and worries are essentially not needed, but their momentum still moves through society.

Our identity is still caught up in striving to do something, to dominate others to feel safe, to be someone to stay secure. To work to fill up our time. It is important to remember that nirvana is not some lofty faraway state or place. It is here and now. We are already free. You cannot create freedom but it can be taken away. Like darkness. You cannot go and create darkness but it can be taken away. You cannot create silence but it can be taken away.

Imagine 20 people in an empty room. If I tell them they have to work out how to get to the other side, but they all have to go across in the same way together, it will probably take them about

10 seconds at the most to decide on single file. If, however, I tell them to go across as a group – but everyone must stick to their own way of crossing – they will remain the whole day arguing and persuading others to go across their way. They may start fighting and hating each other. The simple goal of walking across a room together cannot happen if people's egos remain rigid and they pridefully stick to the way they want things to be.

We could have world peace right now. There is no obstacle to everyone walking hand in hand together. We just don't want it! We can create system after system but it is something within each individual to wake up to. People want to fight. You cannot get rid of hateful discrimination by making it a policy. What feeds discrimination is attention. If you're an interior designer you will notice immediately how your friend's living room is. If you are dwelling in your being, you may not even notice that all the walls are stripped ready to be painted!

If you force people not to discriminate because of hair color, they will discriminate because of shoe size. A group of people are together; someone is from England and so the rest discriminate against him because they are from Scotland. The Scottish people can join together in a friendship of communal hate and discrimination, until they find out one is a Hindu and the rest are Christian. They bond together in hateful discrimination until they find out one is a Protestant and the rest are Catholic. A chorus of joy rings out in their communal bonding, until they find they all like football and support Celtic but one supports Hibernian! They cast him out in joyful togetherness. All is well and even better as they all live in Glasgow until they find out all are from the eastern side but one is from the west. They hate him and bond together in their disapproval until they find out one of them went to a different school from the others and he is soon cast out. All is well again until they realize they live on the opposite side of the street. Both now are content to be miserable alone.

Ironically, a couple from Palestine and Israel are watching all this and laugh at the group because all white Europeans look, sound and act exactly the same!

Discrimination is endless because it is the fearful projection of ego. It is the ego's defense mechanism for existing in separateness. It is the mind calculating and quantifying everything. It is a necessary tool but destroys the world if not transcended. The mind cannot be ignored or bypassed; it must be transcended. One develops an ego; it is part of life. However, in different styles of life throughout the ages there were guidelines and a structure set in place to help go through the ego. These structures themselves became weapons for the ego. They have to be changed again and again. It is amazing to me, but understandable given the limited size of communications in the past, that the guides and helpers of the past didn't have restructural clauses built in. I guess many masters tried. Zen especially has an inbuilt teaching that the teachings are to be let go of.

We must on a personal and societal level be free to ask ourselves – is it working? Do I have the peace I was seeking or am I still restless? Are these teachings giving me joy, love and wonder? Innocently ask.

It is the art of life, and as perennial as the stars to find the inner meaning within the form, to find the spirit and meaning of a rule by not sticking to it rigidly. There will always be those who would rather stick to the structure created to find truth, even if it means losing the truth itself. Essentially, if we stick to the structure we won't get blamed. If we follow the truth and it doesn't work out to how we thought, people will immediately point the finger of blame. But if we just follow the rules, we can breathe easy – even if it means the truth was lost.

Our structures have become magnificent. Our global networks, our tall buildings, our entertainments and entertainment systems, our clever philosophies, our ancient traditions. Everything improving faster and faster, we work harder and harder and progress and progress, but for what? The small and simple truth seems to be trampled on. However, for all the posturings of the global traditions, cultures and materialisms we all know the simple truth: that happiness is found within. Even though we all want a better social structure, that speaks to our times and needs. We all want more personal freedom and a collective peace. Our structure at present – with a rampant negative focused media ready to attack anything or anyone if it means selling more. Something needs to give.

If we stop for one second in laying blame.

If we decide that we as human beings living now are free.

We are free to have inner and outer world peace.

We are free to create any structure we want to help counteract and balance the forces that got us to the material world we're at now.

We are free to slow down and change our economic system.

We are free to create a new structure for finding peace within.

What would happen?

Can we walk across the room together?

Can we use this magnificent material comfort to explore global peace?

What is stopping us?

What is stopping all the world leaders right now from getting together in one room and having the session broadcast live across the world on every TV set and the Internet to sort out world peace?

Can we decide that we don't need more?

Can we recognize that all the material comforts in themselves are not enough?

How difficult will it be to globally decide we can't keep consuming the world's resources as if they are inexhaustible?

No one wants to work in menial jobs all their lives; can we not figure out a way to create a global economy that sustains all our human needs of food, water, air, and shelter as a fundamental basis? The entire population working only on this, the rest of the time is for playful discovery of the inner and outer world.

How hard can it be to walk across a room together?

Who cares who decides how we go across – as long as we go across?

Are we mature enough to have this world as our home? To live in it magnificently, to enjoy outer comfort and find the inner peace of the awakened ones?

No structure can do it but new ones can help breathe new life and bring great happiness and can help get the ego mind under control quicker. The collective ego has run rampant for a while and we know the damage it has done to the world. Can we do something about it? Do we want outer and inner peace or would we prefer to keep the old structures that haven't managed it thus far?

Do we need aliens to come and attack us so we will unify, simply to discriminate and hate, or can we recognize our global humanity now?

It is important to note that being peaceful doesn't mean being physically inactive. You may still fight even in peace. Martial artists are people who channel the urge for physical action into peace and grace. Boxers are as sporting as anyone else.

Violence is the problem.

Violence is the non-consensual interference with another living being.

It can be clearly understood that two people hitting each other on the head can be done in consensual joy. While someone may prevent you from enjoying your own body, *for your own good*, this interference is true violence.

Let us imagine then a world where:

There is a global anthem sung at all sporting events.

There is a global flag of the world: an image of the earth.

On everyone's passport it simply states 'human being.'

The global religion is: seeking the truth.

The global prayer is: sitting together in silence.

Everyone has a house, food, clothes and clean water. The rest of the human work output and creativity is invested in recycling energy so we don't destroy any more of the planet.

Every individual has the right to live however they like as long as it doesn't interfere with another person's physical or internal space. Only when it does, does the society get involved.

Will this structure not be more helpful; do we not yearn for world peace?

How hard can it be?!

We can imagine, also, how much easier it will be and how many problems can be solved with two simple words: birth control.

Can we be scientific with ourselves? Can we take a leap away from the structures built on books written thousands of years ago? Do we need to get into endless debates and arguments or can we not clearly see that if the world's population went down a few billion over the coming years this would be helpful for the food air deal?

Is it up to us or are we going to let people who are dead decide our fate?

Chobo: What is the matter?

A: Well, just all of the fear and insecurity that stops me ever spending time single, I think. Although, I feel it's more like the kind of crisis that can come with transformation.

C: Yes, the consciousness can burp up a lot of shit; I was ill for years recently for no reason the doctors could find! Are you staying present with your presence?

A: Yes, although there are times when I can't feel anything outside of the state. I've been listening to Jon Kabat-Zinn talking about mindfulness, the awareness being bigger than what is happening in it. It makes a lot of sense. I'm learning to bring myself back to the moment.

C: Yes, it is a beautiful practice to keep bringing your power of attention back to the natural presence. But I think you are beyond the need of practice, no? You are the one aware of attention and loss of attention of the 'person' who is practicing mindfulness. This is not to be practiced when you start practicing. There is again a duality of the one who is practicing being oneself.

A: I can almost get my head around that. Or my awareness around it, rather. Do you not think there is work to be done?

C: NO! You are the Buddha. Your consciousness is here/now. The master key is to dis-identify with feeling; you are a body of thoughts. A thought is nothing; but believed in and identified with it has power. But the thought is not self employed, remaining as natural presence. It is a wonderful way to dis-identify. This presence is formless but here, it is SO here, that we miss its obvious continuous presence and cannot believe that presence is the Buddha.

A: Isn't zikr a kind of work, then? I mean 'zikr' in its widest sense, as remembrance.

C: I think there are many paths but, at the end of the day, we must find the pure consciousness called God/Buddha/nirvana etc. and at some point this can't be practiced. There are many teachings of dropping the medicine. Kill the Buddha. This means drop the practice. Effort, effort, effortless, because the mind cannot do it. Papaji used to see Krishna but his master, Ramana, told him he had to drop his path. The train brought him to his destination. Now it is time to let it go.

A: My belief that I am not Buddha right now is pretty strong. Well, it certainly is strong at times.

C: That is it, that is everyone's problem. They can't believe that nirvana is here and now. Life is miserable, so how can anyone who is doing the same things be in bliss?! It's just a thought. Bring your attention back to the one who is aware that they don't believe. Everything is passing, passing, passing through the unchanging.

A: I like the thought of 'being' being free. I like that it's not even a thought. What I meant by zikr was reaffirming, returning until I can believe it.

C: Who is the one returning? And returning to what? These are not cynical questions, but challenging internal truths of ourselves when we constantly put ourselves as a goal.

A: So isn't ourself a goal?

C: Aren't you here?

A: Here I am.

C: Can you practice existing?

A: Of course not!

Truth is no one's providence

What is more beautiful than the color red?

I have yet to receive an answer to this question. In our modern spiritual paradigm, two extremes seem to have unfolded; one is a blasé, quick fire response – 'We are all already enlightened, puh, I KNOW that!' And the other is the global utopian love village, of endless 'new age' therapies to get you there. The two are, of course, connected. People are being bored with enlightenment; 'getting' that we are already that, and are still seeking to find utopia. I have asked many people as they prepare to join another group, or practice another meditation technique, or go out clubbing, or get intoxicated to reach the Goddess: What is more beautiful than the color red? They can't answer, but also don't want to accept the notion of staying here and now. Instead, they would rather keep a quest going, in their minds, of a beautiful world. In fact, many use the teachings of being present *as* the excuse. The often-used Zen story of the seeker coming to the master and the master pouring tea into his cup until it overflowed, showing to the seeker he had too much knowledge in his mind for the truth to fit in, is now itself part of the 'too much' knowledge.

What is more beautiful than the color red? This is Zen mind, beginner's mind. It is to live in wonder at the world around you right now. If you still need to get drunk, intoxicated, find friends, join new groups, have a love affair where you have to persuade people it is just so incredible, be a Goddess, be Tantric, it means you have an intellectual understanding of the truth.

As can be seen, thoughts are very intoxicating and powerful.

If you are doing these things and justifying them with spiritual new age knowledge such as: being enlightened is just being human, you can do anything you want it's all awareness, I'm following my heart, you are befooling yourself and are intoxicated by egotistical knowledge of the spiritual path. You may be so far gone in your arrogance and ignorance you say you are already enlightened, and one does not need to do anything and you are mistaking following whims and living a plush comfortable indulgent lifestyle as being awakened from suffering.

In fact, I have found that true spirituality annoys these types of people. They deny true masters, because you can only do it yourself, but always want to tell other people about it!

What is more beautiful than the color red?

The story is told of the thirsty rich man who would bargain away his whole empire for a bottle of water in the desert, begging the question: 'Is, then, your entire life's efforts the equivalent of a bottle of water?' It is shown as less so. This leads us to what awakening is. It is the ability to know the value of water already. If you are not awake, you are still seeking for something, you are still empire building. The empire maybe a higher social status, such as being a Goddess, more friends, better physical/mental/psychic/occult abilities wherein one feels one will thrive better.

For the awakened one, this world is utterly mysterious and wonder filled, no one could persuade you to be different or have different experiences. The color red is inexpressible, water is unparalleled, sitting in the dark is utterly incredible, sitting in the light is utterly incredible. The world is more beautiful than you could ever imagine and you are more beautiful than you could ever imagine or project yourself to be. You can never project or wish for a better outcome than is already the case.

Freedom

If you need to ask permission to be free, what kind of freedom do you have?

The whole purpose of a master is to help you find your freedom – not enslave you. Like a mother bird escorting her babies out of the nest on their first flight, the true master wants only one thing: for you to fly on your own in the vast sky of life.

The word guru has been translated as 'spiritual guide.' This means someone showing you the way, pointing out different paths of the formless, giving encouragement as one dives into their own being. Guidance does not mean dictation, enslavement, order, or rules and one must be careful of subtle enslavement, such as, 'It is your choice but I'm implying if you don't follow me you will fail, or go to hell.' You are the mystery you are seeking to know and this mystery is just as mysterious for someone outside helping you. Or is it not a mystery for them? Have they solved the unknowableness of life? Buddha said there are as many paths as there are people. No one knows how or when the uncaused will be recognized.

The word 'spiritual' does not mean 'worldly.' A master isn't guiding you with your lifestyle choices either. Do you really want another human being to tell you how and when you should move your left arm? Or when and where you fall in love? Or how many times your penis gets erect in this lifetime? Or if it touches another piece of flesh? This is undignified. You are a Buddha, perhaps unconscious, but not a slave, not someone who needs potty training.

A master is someone who is at peace within. Clearly, we can see the majority of people on this beautiful planet are not at peace, not living in contented bliss. The master has found the unidentified space within. Clearly, we can see people need encouragement to find this space. Instead of queuing up to get a glimpse of professional golfers who are just hitting something with a stick, or people kicking a ball at each other like pigeons chasing a crumb. Or getting excited to meet a friend who, for a lot of people, is just someone you need to vomit your internal dialogue on so that you don't feel insane by talking to inanimate objects. We should not feel lowered or degraded for wanting to meet the one who has seen through the ego and knows joy.

Hopefully we have matured spiritually and we are not seeking a master to stamp our 'never, never land' passport for kissing his ass. It is so obvious to those who have followed the master that it is helpful for dropping one's ego. If you say, 'I don't need an egoless being to help me drop my ego,' who is saying it? For what purpose are you saying it? Is it not the pain of the ego that is felt, and this egotistical pain rejects? If you want to live in love and egoless, why are you saying no to another being? Do you say no to anyone else? Do you say no to a driving instructor? Do you say no to the person who wrote the book saying you don't need a master to be egoless? Do you say no to your friends when they help you have a good time? 'NO! You won't help me have a good time! I want to be spiritual so I must attain it on my own.'

We can see without even going to a master that he is performing his function and starting to mirror your experience. The master/disciple relationship is a sublime form; be careful not to reject it so swiftly, especially if you are still interested in other forms such as worker/boss, friend/enemy; the master/disciple form is unique in that it will end attachment to all forms.

Of course there is room for abuse, as in all forms. However, a lot of the time it merely shows what one was trying to obtain from that relationship. It could be power, social recognition, attention from someone seen as special, hierarchical progression, failing to attain our idea of spiritual states.

Again our minds can be exposed merely by the events going on around a master. If someone is helping the master physically and showing outer devotion, we can get jealous because we think being close means higher prestige. What we really wanted was to be someone special. We can get confused by acts of devotion, thinking it is something the master wants, or we may think it is wrong and is enslaving. While, at the same time, we may feel an act of devotion and kindness ourselves if someone offers us ten thousand pounds. We might want to take them out for dinner or try and repay them some other way. No one, except those who know the within, would think it weird that you bought this person dinner. In fact, if you just took money off someone without being thankful to them, chances are you would be condemned. This spiritual life is formless, invisible, it is known subjectively. When one experiences true joy, the kind that ten thousand pounds promises but doesn't actually deliver, one is thankful to the master for helping one find it. In fact, the master giving you total freedom makes you even more thankful to him.

My mantra is that the way is simple, clear and obvious. We know it very easily in our hearts; it is very natural. We don't need to overthink it. Today, as has been forever, the mind tries to make logic out of the natural and simple. A good example of this happens on the path of people who preach Advaita or non-duality, who confuse the teaching of oneness to mean everything is the same. They call enlightenment a myth and scorn effort, claim there is no need for gurus because we are already that, while they themselves teach!

It is so simple, clear and obvious that some people are wiser than others. We don't need to philosophize, debate, argue, think about it too much; we instinctively know that a suicidal depressed teenager who hates himself is not in the same state of peace as a Buddha. We know that a frantic junkie rapist is not the same as a being unidentified with his body/mind.

Logic and life are not the same. Our small mind is but a fragment of the vast mystery. When logic hears 'everyone is a Buddha,' or we are all one, or you are already that, it tries to figure things out to fit and be in accord with how it thinks. The mind is so stupid, so bent in on itself, it may even say there is no such thing as wise people, because we are all one!

Clearly, the experience of understanding existentially that I am a Buddha, I am. That is different than just understanding about it by reading a book. Otherwise everyone who read the teachings of Buddha would be as peaceful as Buddha (that's a wee bit of logic for you).

All those who attain to that are taught one must find a master; even those rare, rare beings, who attained on their own, taught the master/disciple relationship. And the true masters also taught 'be a light unto yourself' – so evidently it's not about giving up your freedom; it's about giving up your ego.

Another simple, clear and obvious truth that effort is required is that no one (maybe there have been one or two in the history of humanity) has attained and recognized their Buddha nature by never thinking about it. People don't just go to the office, watch football, have a laugh down the pub and naturally become enlightened. There are no droves of people entering samadhi in Newcastle town center. Among the thousands of people I came across there, I barely met a handful of people I would consider happy. Compare that to people who sit at the feet of the awakened ones. It is said of one Tibetan guru, Je Tsongkhapa, that *thousands* of his disciples attained liberation. Thousands of Buddha's disciples awakened. You can find this with many other masters, and even those who didn't fully awaken had great moments of bliss and led joyful lives. Hmm – I wonder if there is a connection between conscious effort to attain to the Self and living your life with no conscious effort about the truth within?

As Bono said, 'We're one, but we're not the same.'

Generally the people who make such 'mindy' comments are the ones without a master.

It is better to say that one must make effort, and one cannot do it with effort. One is already a Buddha, and one is not already a Buddha.

Life is mysterious and not illogical. It is unknowable. It is not a bunch of throwaway comments. 'You don't have to do anything, you're already that.' 'It's all just a dream.' 'Everything is just consciousness.' As if you *know* what *that* is, or what is behind the dream, or what consciousness is. When people make such throwaway comments, it shows their knowledge is borrowed and is coming from their mind. It is their way of trying to figure out life and retain control – as if they know what life is.

The meaning of such statements is not in the words. I had the fortune of studying acting. When you are presented with a script, you really start to understand that the meaning is not on the page. Each rehearsal, each performance changed the meaning as each actor went deeper into themselves. Shakespeare lasts because the meaning is given by the actor and each actor has a different meaning through who he is. Each actor is scintillating, unique, individual and the meaning is different every time, and yet the basic surface level common ground meaning we share on the logic/mind level stays the same. This is what it means to be sensitive and open, to not just turn up to *Macbeth* and say, 'What's the point – I know this!' The meaning of a master saying to you that 'You *are* That!' depends on your sensitivity, receptivity, the master, the timing, the unknown penetrating in. If all the factors are right, just hearing these words one can find the Buddha within. If you are stuck with your knowledge that 'we're all one and everyone is already enlightened' you can remain unenlightened for the rest of your life.

It is so simple, clear and obvious that words can help. They can also hinder. The medicine can be a poison if taken too much. So, words and effort take us up to the point of no effort. We have done all we can do as a doer.

A: I'm moving into the space of being alone without a story. I'm feeling a tendency not to want to socialize. My friend is disappointed that I'm not going to visit him.

Chobo: Yes, others I've spoken to are at this point too. Where the words are falling away and a space is needed to give birth to a new dimension of being. As Mooji would say, zip up the sleeping bag of your being and stay quiet. Relish the opportunity to be alone because it won't last.

A: It is funny you should say that because I think the fear part is that it'll last forever and it'll be too late to come back. I do relish it, very much. Also the thing of appearing to be somebody while actually you know you're not anybody at all, or you want to dwell in your 'nobodiness.' The work that I do is all about being somebody, or trying to be somebody. It's funny. While I've had moments of panic, I've also been enjoying noticing when I don't mind.

C: It is funny; the mind and its tricks. Again, others I've spoken to are having a similar problem of the mind tricking them. A common theme is letting go of trying to save the world! Because they think that if they become enlightened or awake, they will no longer be able to because they will realize everything is perfect!

Somebody trying is the fabric of society. However, if you can rest in your natural presence, you will be able to witness the 'somebody' as just a thought or appearance. It is appearing in the presence and it can be taken as fun. Also it has its function and limitations. 'I am who I am, and that's OK' is recognized from a witnessing consciousness, and there is no problem. Your limitations are the clothes of God.

A: I think, however we are inside, everybody will assume we are somebody anyway. That way it is possible to carry out whatever role without anybody guessing.

C: Yes, it is almost impossible to recognize an awakened being without a ritual.

You Can't Be a Buddha; I Know You!

Nirvana is here and now, it is not something outside ourselves; it is in fact who we are. Our humanity goes deeper than mere person-hood. When scholars got hold of the teaching 'you are not a person' they turned it into 'you are not a human.' It is understandable. How can the experience of nirvana be here and now?! We know life, we are here and we are miserable. How can someone else who is eating a burger next to us be 'in nirvana'? The only way the mind can comprehend it is to make it something other than life, something super-human, not of this world. How can someone you know who is eating the same food as you, going to the same shops, watching TV beside you be in a state of bliss?!

We can see from one aspect that awakening is simply dropping disbelief. It shows truth is within, it is how we are experiencing life; it is not a place or an object of knowledge. Otherwise it could be given to you. If it can be given to you, it can be taken away. But no one can take you away from you. You are life. Whatever is presented before you is not you. You are the witness of everything that happens. Is this true or not? Can you find something that will happen in your life that you will not witness? My master said to me, 'If you are gifted by God with the whole universe, but in exchange you have to give up your consciousness, your perceiving self, is it a good deal?'

Nothing can be added or taken away from your being. Once you begin identifying with That and not the fleeting personality given to you by others, you start to feel the uncaused bliss of being. No one can give it to you, and if they could, would you want it? One's dignity and grace lies in the fact that one is as much himself as anyone else. No one has 'more' consciousness than someone else, or more silence, or is more here and now. You are That which you are seeking.

What was it that made Bodhidharma and the other mystics laugh so much when they woke up? It was that they have always been what they were searching for. Is it not here and now? Did Bodhidharma create a perceiving consciousness? Did his ego make consciousness, or did he simply recognize That which is always there? If he can do it, can you not? Did Lao Tsu exist 'more' than you? Does the pure sense of just existing belong to someone else and their gang? Do you need to be born on a certain continent and have certain clothes and lifestyle to exist? Do you need to be a Buddhist, Hindu, Christian, alien, new age to know that you exist? Is knowing that you exist spiritual, religious, non-religious, political, social? Or is it just life as it is?

Do you need to pray or recite mantras to know that you exist?

The way of truth is neither spiritual nor religious. It does not deny spirituality nor religions. It is simply who you are.

If a child is born among wolves, and knows no human language, and never meets any human beings, and one day she drags another wolf to safety from a fire – risking her own life – is this compassion or not? Is it Christian, Buddhist, Hindu, or atheist? Or is it simply what is? We know from our own experience that if a Buddhist sees the encounter, he will say she was blessed by Buddha; if it is a Christian she was blessed by Jesus, and so on.

We can see clearly that religions and spirituality are caught up with the mind and human conditioning. The truth, however, lies beyond the mind and its conditioning. It has nothing to do with beliefs and dogma. Because it has nothing to do with them, it is not against them either. Because religions and spirituality are expressions of ourselves, they also are manifestations of truth.

With the global communications of today, the world is experiencing an outer oneness. We know clearly that religions are born from a certain cultural paradigm. Religious debates and arguments appear very childish now. However, the human being in its journey of awakening is still electrified by the outer manifestations that call to it of the inner truth. Someone in a monk's robe has a tremendous impact on the psyche. Many times I watched awakened beings ignored – i.e. for someone who was not even on the path, merely because he was wearing robes. Among all the forms of the world, here is one that speaks of transcending forms. It calls to us, to our true being, we feel something. Ritual has an impact. Myths resonate. However, these myths can take new forms. Part of the mythological under-standing and the way of things is we start to cling to the form telling us to drop forms. The masters devise new methods, they keep tricking us, shaking us up. Life doesn't fit into any rules. There is no way to live life; one simply lives it. In the unfolding of it, the truth goes deeper or we stay within our delusions. This is the art of life. It is more a flavor, a feeling, an art form than a set of rules and figuring it out with the mind.

It is also important to remember that the truth is life, and life is everything. Life is also the forms. We can create beautiful forms. Silence and melody. Melody and silence. Knowing ourselves is our birthright. Knowing ourselves is our freedom. Knowing ourselves is no one else's business. Knowing ourselves is nirvana. Knowing ourselves is simply knowing ourselves. We simply look and ask, 'Who am I?' The only way to know who you are is by investigating yourself. It can be very helpful to find a master to help you with your enquiry. If you are reading this, you are seeking help outside of yourself. If you need no help or guidance, you will never read a book. The fact is that even teachers who say you don't need masters are themselves offering help. Help denouncing help but undeniably help nonetheless. Or is it not outside help? Did you invent your own language and conceptions, or did you receive them from someone else? Did you create your own world to live in? Some people don't have the inclination for devotion, but it is unwise to say that help from a master is not needed at all. However, it is only a helping hand or a shout from the sidelines. You must do all the work, you must find yourself. And it is a great journey, a great joy. What is this fighting mind that denounces those who are on the path of devotion? How joyful it is to find the one who is just himself, just being! A true human being. To know that peace is attainable, to dwell in his presence, to just be, to feel the bliss of just being. To feel the mystery of life uncovering itself just by being in the presence of someone just being. To sit with those gathered round the master all seeking the truth; love, joy, peace. Or is it better to watch football, or play Xbox and worship and follow politicians, to get excited because an actor is in your town?

The joy of simply knowing you are a seeker of truth. If we are going to play with forms and delight in them, this is less likely to start fights than others. 'I am a seeker of truth.' This very knowledge can be enough to overcome depression. Those depressed, those who don't see the value of committing their entire life to the outer forms, are often seekers of truth without the knowledge of it. As my master says, 'Life isn't just about paying rent.'

It can be very important to be around other seekers. We need love, it is a deep need, we need to feel we belong. We need to feel there is something else. This something else, this 'saudage,' is the call from within ourselves to find ourselves. If we don't have the culture for it, if our expressions of truth are out of date, the need will make weird manifestations. We end up with people wanting to be Jedis or vampires. The outer expressions calling us are as desperate as fictional film characters and fantasy bonds. I know some adults who *still* want to be a Jedi! They are happier to follow the made-up characters of a mediocre filmmaker's fantasy than find the healthier forms of truth seekers.

The family of truth seekers is a beautiful experience and need. It is a chance to express love, to show ourselves, to make mistakes and be vulnerable. As Joseph Campbell says, 'We are not seeking the meaning of life, we are seeking a deep experience of life.' Life has no inherent meaning. We are life. The deeper we go, the more significance it has. There is nothing wrong with watching TV, but if that's all we do, we will feel empty. There is nothing wrong with believing in 'la la land' where you will get 18 hundred virgins licking your gonads when you die, or there is an alien planet 18 hundred light years away where unicorns ride in the sky, but if that's all you do, you will feel unsatisfied. Otherwise, everyone that believed would be at peace, instead of fighting or looking elsewhere. However, those that know themselves have found that satisfaction. In the history of seeking, no master has started believing something else.

The experience of making bonds with truth seekers is helpful. It is not about feeling doe-eyed all day; it is about seeking truth. What covers our true selves can often be very ugly. The process of getting rid of our delusions and inner dirt is not necessarily a pleasant one. It can almost be a rule of thumb that if someone is trying to convert you, it means he doesn't know the path because you wouldn't wish it on anyone. The master shares for those who are on the journey. It is a hard journey for many seekers and the master is like a nurse helping and comforting. The nurse may do stuff to you you don't like, such as stick a needle in your arm or cut you open.

Sometimes the family of seekers around a master is like an asylum. Everyone is confronting their demons and madnesses they carry with them. They are looking at what makes them miserable and the difficulty is that they have believed it was the very thing making them happy.

There is also a time and a place for friends. Papaji said, 'I don't have any friends and I don't want any friends.' My master added, 'I just have a friendliness towards everyone.' We often want *friends* in the same way we don't just want a love partner, but a 'twin flame.' We project our desires on to others and confuse causal bliss with the uncaused bliss of knowing oneself. As we go on this journey back home to ourselves, the path becomes narrower and narrower until we are simply dwelling in aloneness. Friends are just humans and at times get jealous. Although outwardly the sangha may say, 'May everyone be happy and live in peace.' When you find yourself dwelling in peace, members of the sangha can be the first to be upset by it. Friends become uncomfortable and some may even hate you for it. When this happens, it can be better just to move alone. The time for friends has passed; your own being is the only thing you need, you are recognizing the Buddha within. Others who think they know you can now be an unnecessary obstacle. It is better to just be quiet, keep it secret, keep it safe. How can someone they know be a Buddha! Regardless, if you have been searching together for years, it can be too much for some to take that you have found That. This shows that their ideas of a Buddha are still linked to fantasy, still linked to outer ideas, outer behavior. A Buddha, for example, has a special hold on others, he can duck before a sword strikes him from behind! If we are seeking occult powers, and a special persona, we will never attain. The truth is somehow very quiet, soft, obvious; it loves life, it is life. It is not seeking a goddess mate. It is not 'I am, and I am you who fits with my lifestyle.' There is nothing more beautiful than the color blue. There is no other world to go to; there is no other lover to find. Just being is enough. Life is bliss. You are life; you are bliss. Everything that appears before you is mysterious and wonderful. One is content. If you are seeking super duper dakini eyeball woman, you are not content. You are seeking a cause for your bliss. You have not attained to That. To yourself. Meeting another lover will not do it. The lover in front of you is enough. Love is very soft and quiet. The big dramatic twin flamers who will scorch the world with their love, will cure the world, will make the world awakened according to their projections of love, somehow just don't feel right. They often talk about the here and now, and 'I know the Advaita teachings and they just don't do it for me.' They are restless in their being. They need adventure, excitement, an other worldly love affair, they lift veil after veil, they uncover and uncover, they have the best dance ever again and again, but somehow they just haven't found peace within. When you find peace within, you eat when you're hungry, and sleep when tired. Everything that happens is more than enough. The world is more beautiful than any of the dakini/goddess/heavenly fantasies.

It is a blessing in disguise that truth and being ordinary go together because you can just get on with your life undisturbed. If you want ego drama, then you want a special super mega astral lover. If you don't and you are quietly content, love will happen very naturally with no effort and no drama. It is love! It is as perennial as the stars; everyone feels this love. I would say that the Tantric lovers often miss it because they are so busy chasing love and bliss, their egos are so bowled over by how AMAZING their love affair is that, apart from themselves, everyone else can smell something egotistical going on.

Being a Buddha can wind up your friends! 'You can't say you existentially know that you know nothing because that's what Socrates said.' Of course, how can someone you know have attained to the same thing that super-human Socrates did? He wasn't like us, was he? This is another reason why we need a master. We need an element of the unknown. Our lives are not blissful and someone who seems to be living the same life and has been near me for 10 years can't be blissful. He can't be getting that bliss from life because I'm living the same life! A master has a necessary distance from which to bang out the disbelief in you that you, yes you, are already That. That life is perfect as it is. That you are a Buddha. Although you may not feel like it! It is simply a matter of recognizing that which is. It is not about creating a super structured ego, or visualizing a body made out of light cheese, or somehow with your mind creating a super-human consciousness, or joining a special Tantra massage bonding group. It is simply looking within yourself and seeing who you are. Twin flames and mega consciousness dakinis may be the way to save the universe; that is for others to pursue and enjoy. Ours is simply recognizing what is, very simply, softly, quietly. In Asia, this path of simple truth, of seeing what is, of being with life right now as it is, was called Zen. We often need to give a name to something, even if that thing is a 'nothing.' We call people who don't follow beliefs, who don't want a label, who don't cling to names, Sufis. For our times of global awareness, it is better to drop the colloquial names and simply call them 'truth seekers.'

A: My I-entity reckons it's bored.

Chobo: Really! That beautiful boredom is the stepping-stone of grace. Boredom is an indicator that the mind is still seeking something; it still feels that somewhere else and something else will be a better place.

A: It still thinks there might be a jury meeting somewhere to decide if it is a failure. And that even this place might be preferable to that place!

C: I didn't understand the first part. Wherever you go, you will be here; this is a 'way in' to your being. Someone said recently, and they were being a spiritual wise ass, that just being consciousness is boring so they like to be in the world. Basically they used this as an excuse for the mind to do what it wants. If your consciousness or beingness is boring, there is no liberation. Your being itself is free, bliss, joy; just rest in it and watch the mind squirm, be happy just to watch it squirm. At some point, one simply has to trust in being utterly simple, and here and now.

A: I am very happy that that is what I want. Even the trouble seems to be a friend, a true friend wearing a funny costume to help me. Thank God my boyfriend doesn't want me. Thank God I live in a boring corner of the world.

C: That's it!

To be a seeker

A seeker is one who is open. Who is experiencing life here and now. A seeker is neither religious, spiritual nor atheist. He or she or it (who knows we may have alien seekers here soon) is investigating all of life; outer and inner. The form and the formless. All of it is part of life. Can any part of life be larger than life? Can life be spiritual? Or is spirituality not an aspect of life? It is a tremendous joy to recognize oneself as a seeker. To feel that life is an exploration, the truth is within us, we are part of life, we are life, we belong. We carry inside us a treasure of great joy. The journey of meditation is an extraordinary one full of wonder and surprise. It is our birthright. Many have gone before us on this journey and they have found out who they are. Many faded away into bliss and silence. Fortunately others tried in various ways to explain and show us that it is possible to be at peace, content, joyous and blissful. That it is our nature. That love is the name we give to ourselves when we move in the world of form. Love is as natural as ourselves. When we find ourselves, we are love. We need not make it a practice; we need not practice virtues. What a relief! As a seeker, one must trust this is true, this trust is born from the presence of a one who knows, or from a deep intuition inside ourselves that we know this. Trust is like an echo of ourselves. It is not belief. Trust is in the realm of feeling. When we fall in love, we trust this feeling. We don't know the outcome of our feelings. If we want outcomes, we don't know what trust is. Externally, the results may not be to our mind's content, but the trust in our feelings or intuition is more fulfilling than whether we managed to rub one piece of our skin on someone else's skin.

Belief is like David Williamson saying, 'That was a good film.' Now, do you know whether it was a good film or not? Of course not, the words have no meaning in themselves! You can believe him but you have no idea if he is lying or if he has even seen the film. If your best friend implores you to see the movie, telling you that you will totally love it, you trust it will be a good film. You still don't know, but in a sense you do know – but you don't. Human communication is deep and mysterious. Every person we meet is different; every encounter reveals a new aspect of life if we are open and receptive. Every area has a different flavor of energy. In the world of Zen, the seeker would move from one master to another, seeking the one he fell in love with. There was no guilt; there was freedom. There was the joy of differences. The magic of unique beings. Every encounter unique, every way special. This is our time. This can be our world. Seeking inside ourselves, meeting others who know how to just be, delighting in sharing this treasure. Not trying to change the world according to our ideas, but just living life with joy and trusting life.

When I was with my first master, I had to remind people again and again of the title of his main book, *Joyful Path of Good Fortune*, which was essentially a commentary on the book *Liberation in the Palm of Your Hand*. These two titles are the flavor of the seeker. Joy and truth within. It is life! It is about laughter, joy, fun, daring, sex, exploration, emotion, calm, silence. It is about being human and your right to be as you are. Not even your right, you are as you are. It is about dropping labels and conditions given by others; any information given to you is not you. Who is the one that was born and knew life before language? Is that one spiritual? Religious? American? Pakistani? What if they were born on a boat, 'Atlantian'? Or are they simply just a human being?

In the spiritual and religious world, they often talk about the difference between us and animals. That we can be religious and they can't and so on, but we have to define religion in such statements. In my experience, animals are kinder, more sensitive, more patient and loving than human beings. They don't destroy the planet, and thus they seem to be more intelligent. They don't deny or indulge their sexuality, thus making them more natural. Human beings, it seems, are far lower qualitatively than animals. Yes, we know how to kill better in more sophisticated ways, but that shows how dangerous our intellect is and what depths of stupidity pride and ego will take. There are two things to me which seem uniquely human which are our great gifts; and they are laughter and being aware of awareness. People who can laugh, who don't take life as a serious affair and who know themselves don't start wars, don't dominate others, don't kill for their religion or beliefs.

The seeker has no beliefs; he is open and trusts his feelings. His religion is life, his God is life, he makes no divisions of nations as he sees the world is one and we are all human beings. Life itself reveals how to live, and he trusts life. If you put your hand in the fire, you get burnt. He does not condemn life, he does not think it is a sin to be alive. He does not think the world is wrong and being human is wrong, and we only find happiness when we die. This world is the world he is in. He does not know about another world. He wants to be in this world now. He does not deny his body, he does not deny his mind, he wants to know who am I.

If my body is in a cold or a hot room, how will it change who I am?

If I move my left arm first? If I put my penis over here or over there? If I eat something thick or something thin? How will these bodily movements affect my truth of knowing who am I?

If seven thoughts float through my brain or 21 thoughts, how does that affect my inner awareness? The witness watches a thought about finding the twin flame or England's chances in the World Cup; am I suddenly more or less the witness?

Of course, if I am identified with my body, then it will matter and I will become more or less miserable; likewise if I am identified with my thoughts then either of the above thoughts will excite me and thus make me suffer. The question is of identification, not body or mind.

A: What is the mind's true purpose? Surely it is not here only to trick us?

Chobo: Why do you need a purpose? THAT is the trick of the mind. Are you trying to place life into a conceptual box? Are you hoping to have stuff figured out if you find your being? What can be more beautiful than a Buddha's mind? So it is not the mind that is a problem in and of itself. It is our glory that we can go astray and suffer. Suffering is the growing pains of consciousness.

A: No, I don't need a purpose. Does that mean my mind and body don't need one either?

C: The birth of Zen was Buddha sitting with a flower; what purpose does a flower have? Jesus said the lilies are more beautiful than Solomon, i.e. existing here and now is more beautiful than any ideas about existing here and now. Without the mind there is no transcendence, but it is not the mind that is the place of transcendence.

A: Anyway, I don't need to know this now.

C: Okay.

A: I mean, the question about mind doesn't need to be answered, it was only cos I started feeling sorry for it!

(laughter)

And you said you loved it so much and then I did too. Oh, poor mind, I'll find you another job!

C: But you're right and it is a very delicate point, that the mind is not an enemy and one doesn't get rid of anything in transcendence, but if you don't recognize its faults, it will keep you in suffering.

A: Which is why I like the image of mind-sufferings being a friend in a funny costume. And all these events which my mind doesn't like, such as waking up in the morning!

C: Now let's head back again... Who is the one saying, 'I like the image of mind-sufferings being a friend.' Can you recognize that one? Is that one findable? And who will be the one looking for it?

A: That is the one that has to have something to say, that wants in on the party when it sees a bit of bliss going on. So who is THIS one?

C: Is it a person?

A: Just some thoughts.

C: Do you not recognize the thoughts? Can a thought recognize itself?

A: Thoughts don't have their own being.

C: So you can't be 'just some thoughts,' yes?

A: I can't be that.

C: Who is saying, 'I can't be that'?

A: The thinker who I am aware of? It feels like there is a thinking entity, but that can't exist on its own.

C: Great, let's slow down and confirm: you know you are not your thoughts.

A: I do.

C: You know that you are aware that there is a thinker, so you can't be that. You know you are here, you know you are existing. Can that which is aware be seen? Or is it simply witnessing without being a somebody witnessing?

A: Awareness seems to be able to perceive awareness.

C: Can it?

(long silence)

I like the silence.

(laughter)

Has this awareness ever been not part of your life?

A: Of course not, it is older than this body and totally fresh.

C: Now all the 'practice' is simply being this awareness that is here effortlessly, 24/7. That means all the thoughts of the universe can come, but you KNOW you are separate from them and you KNOW you are separate from the old sense of I based on personality. That is it. Liberation. Simple. Done.

A: Liberation, but 'Buddhahood'?

C: *(laughter)*

Oh the mind! '... But I read this book, and it says it's this shape, and you will be able to fart wine.'

(laughter)

Believe me, I know those doubts. I hope I can say this to you now, and you will take it in the right spirit. When you can drop the fantastical, you can see things differently. I read an apparent saint, Ibn Arabi, his book, and it was a pile of rot, there was nothing spiritual in it. Just fantastical desires. These are the kinds of texts the Zen people say we must burn.

A: I doubt that they are rot!

C: It's the kind of austerity-based wonder that people equate with spirituality. I say this in light of your words, because we have fantastical ideas of liberation, and those ideas prevent us from seeing what is, and we constantly remain in doubt, we may still be looking for 'something to happen.' Do you think liberation is outside of your being?

A: I don't think liberation is a place to be inside or outside anything. Maybe I still see it as a destination, though. To be liberated, you must have been unfree.

C: Are you unfree? Is liberation separate from who you are?

A: Freedom IS who I am.

C: And you are here/now, or not?

A: I am here.

C: So why do you doubt your freedom and ask if there is a 'Buddhahood' beyond this?

A: But what about all that bliss?

C: *(laughter)*

Now we get to the desire! See what happens for a while if you forget all about bliss and trying to get anything at all, and totally be who you are right now, and feel your being is all there is. We will chat again soon.

A: Okay.

Non-Identification is the Key

As long as we are identified with either our body or mind, we will be miserable. Why? Because we are identifying with what we are not.

The master key to meditation and truth and happiness is to find the witness, the inner seer. We do this by asking the question, 'Who am I?' This is our own journey, our own truth, it is beyond labels because all labels are outside ourselves. We begin.

Who am I? Am I my body? It seems like I am, if someone punches me I feel pain. I look in the mirror and see me. If I want to go over there, it is my body that must go. If someone calls me an asshole, I get upset. If someone says I'm ugly, it affects me!

Do you feel like this?

First questions for you: Is there a one who witnesses the pain? Is it the body itself that recognizes the one in the mirror or is it the one called 'me'? Can a dead body notice and feel upset by insults, or is something else needed for that to be recognized?

If I get a haircut, I feel different. If I wear new clothes, I have a different sense of identity. When I was younger I had a different identity, a different sense of I than now.

Do you feel like this?

Is there not, however, a sense inside that I have never changed? That both things seem to happen, that my identity constantly changes, and yet there is a sense of something unchanging?

This ever-shifting identity we call 'ego.' It is the mind's reflection or, as my master says, the 'ever-changing self-portrait' of the composite elements of everything we are identifying with. It is the picture or appearance that emerges from lots of colored dots on a screen. Or all the paint strokes produce an image that rises out of all the colors. Our awareness perceives our body and an image arises of a person; it is what the mind does. It sees lots of pieces of metal, and a car appears to the mind's eye. The person, of course, goes deeper; not only is it the body, but it is the identification with the mind and emotions too that makes the portrait so deep.

We start with the body because it is generally easier to separate the witness from the physical form. We enquire again and again, am I my body or am I witnessing my body? Can the body witness itself without consciousness? If something happens to my body, am I any less? We use our power of imagination to help our enquiry. Imagine we have been anesthetized by the doctor. We can't feel a thing and our eyes are closed. The doctor informs us he has cut our hair off; is our sense of being, of witnessing, of knowing, diminished? He tells us he has cut our leg off; is the witness still not the same? He cuts the other leg off, and then our arms; are we still not existing in the same way? If we are a body, how can we still remain the same if most of our body has been cut off, and if we are the body, we must be diminished? If we stay in the space that is witnessing, how will we suffer? If we, once opening our eyes, start to identify with the body and then say, 'Oh no, I can't do anything!' will suffering not then have started with the identification, and our projected usage and desires in the world? If I am the body, how can I witness parts of it falling off? How can I move in and out of identification with myself? When am I not myself? Am I not the one witnessing that I am not myself?

We can now do the same enquiry with our thoughts.

Do my thoughts exist without me? If I can see my thoughts, I can't *be* my thoughts. Are different thoughts not coming and going? If they are coming and going then who is the one watching them come and go, and can that be identical to the thoughts themselves? Are they not *my* thoughts?

We can go deeper with feelings.

Am I not the one who witnesses feelings? Do feelings not

come and go, and I remain as a witness to the different comings and goings? Does happiness and sadness not come and go, and I am the one who watches that happen? No matter how strong a feeling may be, is it still not witnessed?

Deeper still.

I have a sense of self but do I not witness that sense of self? The self that changes with haircuts, bad thoughts/good thoughts, happiness/sadness – is it not a mere appearance? Can I not see it or talk about this self or ego? Do I not say my ego is hurt? Is it not a phenomenon I can see? Do I not see my sense of self-changing when my body/mind is hurt? If so, how can I be that? Am I not the witness to the sense of self? Do I not notice it? Is it not just a mixture of my body and mind? An appearance? A thought itself? I am the witness of the ego.

Who am I?

Do I have to see myself to know that I exist?

Can this witness be seen?

Who is the one recognizing that the body, thoughts, emotions and ego are seen? Can this one itself be seen?

This question is not to be answered by the mind, but existentially, non-phenomenally, felt within.

The enquiry into truth is a beautiful journey and after a while starts to take a life and power of its own until we finally jump the final Zen barrier and meditation itself is not required.

There are wonderful methods to help the seeker. My master says, 'Stay as eyes only, as if you are just a pair of floating eyes in the world, observing but making no judgments on the world.' These eyes are reflected inwards too; one simply observes that one is now getting angry, that now the anger is fading, and now lots of thoughts are there, now another strong emotion. One stays centered, an observer, the witness.

One can stay as 'I am.'

It is very important to note that this is not an intellectual exercise. As a truth seeker, one must be careful about dismissing any part of life. There is an old saying: 'Be careful what you wish for, you might just get it.' Have you ever thought that it IS life that is forbidding you? And, on looking back, you thank grace that you didn't get what you wished for when you were 10 years old, then 14, and thankfully those wishes at 20, about how the world should be run and what justice is, were thwarted too. Until eventually you realize maybe the person I am right now doesn't know what's best too? Maybe it's Life looking after me that stops me getting what I think about and desire? Even though, right now, they SEEM loving and true? Maybe, like the Buddhas say, it's not until I stop wishing and thinking how I and the world should be, that I will find what it is that I am meant to have?

We are not setting out to destroy our mind or our life energy. We are not in any way, shape or form denying our humanity. On the contrary, as a seeker, one must live life fully; this is not quite true. One is a human being and one is living life. One can believe in rocks being God, one can say everything is not real, one can suppress their sexual energy but it cannot be denied that all of the above is not separate from life. One has to be in order to deny being.

It is simple, clear and obvious that talking to a human being is different than talking to... I cannot say an empty space, because that would be something. I cannot even say nothing because one would be perceiving a concept of nothing. We cannot talk about something that doesn't exist simply because it doesn't exist. It is very easy to become intellectual. It is advised by the Buddhas in many ways to drop this philosophizing of life, to simply be. They talk of cutting off your head, finding your heart, being playful, being childlike – it is all to stop one thinking that the truth can be figured out with your mind. Indeed, if one is too 'mindy' and clever it will make one miserable and one will never attain to the truth.

Life *is*. If there is no such thing as life, who or what is perceiving there is no such thing as life? For the seeker the question is: what is life? Is life separate from me? Can life be if I am not there to perceive it? Am I not life itself? Who am I? Who is the one perceiving life?

All the questions in the enquiry must happen in the here and now existentially, not intellectually. We begin with the mind asking the question. Remember, we do not want to have the attitude of destroying; we do not want to destroy the mind. For one, it presumes a knowledge that the mind needs to be destroyed. It is better to enquire first then decide if you want to destroy your mind. As I said, be careful of what you wish for. We may have an idea that sex or the life force moving through us as sexual energy is 'bad.' We may try and even wish to get rid of it, but when we start the journey within we can have moments of regret for such attitudes, that the things we have denied within ourselves are actually very, very innocent and our denying of them has taken away aspects of our humanity, growth and unfolding.

A Zen master said, 'I eat when I'm hungry, I sleep when I'm tired.' This line contains the entire path of truth. One of the meanings is: one must look after the needs of the body, not to dismiss your humanity as it is. If you stop trying to 'expand,' you will find quite naturally the well within is fathomless and the idea to expand actually prevents the depths of being unfolding out.

The mind is like a giant fishing net. For the Buddha, he quite happily picks it up and throws it into the sea to catch fish when he is hungry. For the one who isn't master of himself, it is as though he gets drunk and becomes totally entangled in the net, hanging in the air; for some they can barely even breathe and move without this net cutting into their skin! The enquiry is like a knife. The knife, however, is stuck on your belt and in order to reach it you have to pull the net in folds. This may even sting and hurt even more than if you just stay hanging in the net, but you have to use the very thing hurting you at the moment to get to the thing that will free you. The master is one who tells you there is a knife on your belt and encourages you to take some pain in order to reach it. Once you have the knife there is another problem. You are blind to how far you will fall once you cut the net. Even though you hung the net in the tree, your drunkenness has somehow made you forgetful. The master is the friend who tells you that it's OK; the fall won't hurt you. You may feel fear but those who trust their friend will go on despite the fear. Once you are out of the net, you can then happily pick it up again and start fishing with it. Maybe you would like a little bit of time to sober up first, and if the net has been especially tight, the joy of being initially free might have some momentary intoxication of its own.

The net is innocent. The mind itself is innocent. At the moment the mind may be cutting us, but all we must do is find the Buddha within and the mind becomes our servant again, not the master. And it is a beautiful servant! How beautiful a thing is the mind of Buddha!

So, the seeking begins ever so gently with the mind. Who am I? We may even internally use the mind, 'OK, I am not the body,' but as we say this, we become aware that 'something' is looking and witnessing that we are not the body and that the words are accompanying the witness. Eventually, this looking and recognition happens without the mind. One sees one is not the body; no squeezing is needed. It is vital not to internally squeeze and push and hurt yourself with the intellect. There is every chance the intellect will start hurting because it is in the hands of the ego. Who is the one looking, in the beginning? It is the ego; it is our current sense of self, the personal self who is looking in order to attain something. Either a spiritual or special state, maybe just trying to find some happiness. Eventually we reach the absurd state of the ego trying to see its own absence and claim that experience: 'Look there's my absence over there! I have attained my absence!' This experience, of someone experiencing an absence, is felt by seekers as a coming and going. The experience inevitably ends with 'then...' or 'but...' – the question is, who is the one seeing there is no ego? Who is saying, 'I got it!'? Who is that one, is it still a personality? Can it be seen? If it can be seen, by whom is it seen? One must not try to give intellectual answers to these questions. As we get used to the questions and the enquiry, the mind aspect drops and we simply look and observe.

We are here and now. Are you not here and now? Without bringing in the past, who are you right now? No thinking is required for you to recognize you are here and now; you know that you are existing. No need to think about it, no need to think about your past, or God, or Buddha, or anything, there is no need to think about a goddess or the tax bill to know that you are existing right now. There is a body here and now that you can perceive. You are not the body, you are perceiving the body – no need to think about it. Is it true or not that you are perceiving the body? Pain may be moving through the body and you can perceive the pain, however, you were there before the pain arose and you continue perceiving after the pain is gone. Therefore, you cannot be the pain because it comes and goes within your perception. Is there any need to think about this or can you simply observe this? The pain may even give rise to thoughts of 'of course I'm the body – I'm feeling pain!' You were there perceiving life before this thought arose and you watch it disappear, so you cannot be that thought. Thoughts keep coming and going but you are watching them. Your attention gets entangled in the thought that you cannot do this enquiry but you are aware that you were not entangled, got entangled and that the entanglement passed. There is no need to think about this; one can simply watch that it happens. If it can be watched, it cannot be you. You may fluctuate between doing well in the enquiry and getting lost in thoughts, a sense of a self succeeding and failing is watched. An appearance of a person who is doing the enquiry is watched. There is merely a sense of existing, an 'am-ness'; this too is watched. Can the one who is witnessing even the sense of just existing be seen?

I Am

Q: How much 'ego' do you need?

A: Just enough so that you don't step in front of a bus.
~ Shunryu Suzuki

The 'I am' is a sublime method.

Life is not a spiritual practice; the enquiry is simply finding out who you are all of the time. It is not something you do. One doesn't do life. One is existing; one isn't making one's own existence. When one is born one isn't making oneself breathe or beat one's heart, one is simply alive. Who is the one that was born, before a name or religion or human concepts were given to it? The sense that one exists is the sense 'I am.' One doesn't need to say 'I am' to know that one exists. Stay with this feeling of 'am-ness.' As you stay more and more with a sense of just 'being,' the enquiry starts to naturally happen spontaneously and constantly. The 'I am' is always here and now. We may have practiced trying to be in the moment. And sometimes it feels easy when we have a materialistic and comfortable lifestyle. Being in the moment translates as getting good feelings, doing what you want when you want, as long as everything is suitably comfortable. We can easily become victims of our arrogance and be blasé with people. We use 'being in the moment' and 'following our hearts' to gain control over others, to avoid difficulty, to be insensitive to others' requirements. If we have to get money, suddenly these excuses of not meeting people or following your heart disappear, and you will turn up at work no matter how you're feeling. You start wanting the moment to be different than what it is. Deep down, underneath the ego's posturing and divine personality, there is a sense of wanting and restlessness. And there is a sense that 'someone' (our ego) is being in the moment.

When we start dwelling in 'I am,' this becomes our center. We have always been who we are but now the illusion of ego is no longer preventing us from seeing it. We are the treasure we always sought. Life takes on the quality of quiet bliss. There is a sense that nothing can be added or taken away from us. Someone comes round who you like, they go away again, but 'I am.' You stand over on that street or you stand over on the other street. One street is red, one is blue. One gives a certain feeling, the other gives a different feeling, but inside 'I am'; it is the same I am. Your being remains the same. When your being remains the same, the objects and experiences and feelings and people's gossip about them become secondary to this constant sense 'I am,' and none of them can change or add to the being. It is not that it is easy to stay in the moment because there is no moment; one simply is and always is. This 'is' is bliss. This 'is' is love. Someone buys you a car, you are still I am. You drive the car, you are still I am. You may even try and deny that the experience of driving a car is affecting you, you are still I am. Someone takes the car away, you are still I am. You sit down to enquire, you are still I am. Can this I am be witnessed? What is witnessing I am? Is that always with I am?

Does this sense of existing, of 'am-ness' require any effort? Do you need to do something to know you exist? If you do something, is it not happening in the sense of existence itself? Can you do something outside the sense of existing? This 'I am' is the effortlessness we seek. We yearn for effortlessness because we know intuitively that that is our nature and that true peace must be effortless, uncreated. As Buddha is quoted to have said, 'All produced phenomena are impermanent.' If we create our peace, then it cannot last. We know this. If we are creating and making effort, we know it cannot last eternally and if we are 'doing' these things, this is what Buddha meant when he said we make life a suffering. It means we are still interested, involved and attached to the comings and goings. These coming and goings may be incredible to the mind's and emotion's ideas, like a divine lover who ticks all the Tantric boxes, or being a supernatural teacher who never makes a mistake and has a magical sway with his students, or turning into a red goddess, or bringing down a political party, or having the best friends in the world. But no matter how hard we try, these things simply come and go, and one has not found the true peace within.

There is another magical element of 'I am.' As said before, we are seeking and investigating life, not denying it. Life is. All of life is. The forms are as much part of life as anything else. One of the points is that for many the forms are all; that there is no such thing as a peaceful within. Life just sucks! It can be helpful to have a break from forms because that has been where we were totally identified, and because we were totally identified with material gain that is where the flow of our suffering occurs. The forms are innocent, a tree is innocent, a car is innocent, but if we have invested all our life's energy so far into having good material objects, such as a good job, hot partner, spiritual recognition, we will suffer from them if we don't find ourselves. Some people even get angry if they don't get the right brand of chopped tomatoes or tinned beans. This shows a deep connection between one's happiness and forms. It can be very easy to fool ourselves when we are living in total material comfort; we live better than kings and queens of old, in fact I would say the average person in the UK is better off materially than the Queen of England. She doesn't have access to that much better quality of food or entertainments and she has zero external freedom. We may think we are spiritual, but when we're suddenly away from our material comforts and have lost our personal space, we find we get just as upset as anyone else. We also find we can use words like Tantra, or quote Osho as a subtle excuse to cling to our materialistic lifestyle, while fooling ourselves that we are going to change the world with our love when in fact we get upset if someone takes something from our fridge. We are overwhelmed with abundance but still can't freely share food; it still doesn't quite satisfy us having the entire world as a marketplace. This is what Buddha meant when he talked about hungry ghosts. That even animals can share and enjoy their shelter and food, while those humans – who are stocked up in their relatively large and comfortable houses – still can't freely share and enjoy it.

To highlight this addiction to comfort and materialism, it can be very helpful to go on retreat, to take a break from the forms, to give a little space for the inner world to be recognized. If you don't make an effort to recognize and find the effortless space, you will stay forever bound within the whims of ego and it's an endless quest for the 'other.'

Once we dwell in 'I am,' once we are steady within, we have no problem with the world – in fact, it becomes a sweet delight. This space is so vibrant, it is not a necessity to move oneself from the world. We are not denying life. We are not denying going on retreat nor denying *not* going on retreat. There is no rule to life. You are life and you are the meaning of life. One can dance, and play, and bake cakes, write poetry, go for long distant walks, go to parties, work in an office. It doesn't give you any more 'beingness.' There is no more sense of existence to be added. It simply doesn't affect who you are. Even if all the magical elves ever imagined came to tickle your toes, you are still 'I am.' You are the witness of everything. You precede all knowledge because you are the witness of it. The magic is, that, there is no need to give up your collection of expensive shoes, or finding your twin flame, and while not giving them up one starts to find the Buddha within. When one does, these things fall away quite naturally. If you try too hard to get rid of material forms, you will simply suffer. This can be a great experience and personal experiment too. There are indeed moments and glimpses where one sees through the world of forms and one wants to give up everything and find the truth. This is beautiful too. For others, that's the last thing in the world they would want to do. The idea of leaving friends and not going to parties and not socializing is abhorrent! When you find peace within, you can chuckle and see that if someone were to tell you before you start the great journey of no journey that you won't have any *personal friendships*, no interest in going out, or doing anything, or being anyone, or having any opinion, of ever being noticed, you know you wouldn't even start it. There is no need to worry. One simply sits and the leaves fall to the ground by themselves. The falling leaf is beautiful too.

The Advaita dilemma

Many modern Advaita practitioners have fallen into the extreme of wisdom. Many have become stuck in Advaita clarity. 'I am That.' It is so simple and obvious. 'Enlightenment cannot be attained.' It is profound and resonates with the mind so well. 'You don't need to do anything, you are already a Buddha.' 'There are no such things as masters, enlightenment is a myth, everything already is.' This would be great – if the truth followed logic and the workings of the mind. Actually, thank God, the truth doesn't. It cannot be contained by *any* philosophy or system of thought. Or can it? Has the truth ever been captured by the mind? The modern Advaitas can be quite arrogant in their dismissals of 'practices.'

If we agree that the truth is beyond systems of thought, that life is a mystery to be lived and not a certitude, that 'It's all just consciousness' (which I've heard many times before in such subtle derogatory tones, proclaiming an arrogance that one has 'figured out' life). When one starts to understand that life is all just consciousness, one is struck almost dumb with silence and profound wonder at the utter inconceivable magnificence and unknowability of life. Everything you see is a source of wonder and mystery; never mind the inconceivable mystery of another human being!

If we agree to investigate life and truth not just with our minds but with our hearts – with a full bottle of paradoxical sauce to be thrown on everything! To playfully look and challenge and wonder.

We can start to find not the truth through words, but exquisite hints. The poeticalness of our being can come alive and dance.

If we are sinking into the 'I am' and we understand deeper and deeper that life is the heart of our subjective experience. We feel more and more that truth is a formless flavor that is bound to us as an inseparable separate.

We talked before about how the impact of truth depends on us and on who is saying their truth. If one has never met a master before, this will be more difficult to understand. But we can. If you are about to have a baby, who will you take advice from: a woman who has had four children or a man who has read a book on how to deliver and raise a baby? They may even say exactly the same words to you, but the impact of their truth is dependent on their being. The being at its core may be formless but life isn't *just* formless. If it were, there would be no difference between the man and woman. But there is a difference. The difference is not objectively measurable but is contained in the realm of felt experience. The interactions and connections and resultant understandings arising are mysterious and unpredictable; they can't be seen by the human eye. This, however, doesn't mean they mean nothing or don't exist.

The difference between an awakened one and someone not awakened is the biggest and most fundamental difference possible. The Buddha doesn't suffer. Maybe to some smart arse Advaitins, they can dismiss where people are at in an offhand manner, and teach that there are no such things as masters and that enlightenment doesn't exist, but to me, seeing fellow humans suffering matters. The teachings of non-duality when in accord are so powerful because they make your compassion even deeper, because what people suffer from is all an illusion.

The truth is very simple, clear and obvious, that people don't want to suffer, and someone who has transcended suffering is, to some degree, different from someone who is suffering.

The Buddha gave a beautiful analogy that our true nature is like the sky and our mind is like clouds covering the blue sky. The problem is not to create a blue sky; it is for the clouds to disperse and the sky will be seen to shine blue. In the past, spirituality fell into the trap of thinking one needs to create a special enlightened consciousness. Today, the extreme is in thinking the clouds don't exist or matter at all. Life, remember, is everything and it is mysterious and deep. We now need to think of this analogy in terms of effect from the point of view of a person born under black clouds.

Is there a difference in life from when the sky is full of black clouds than when the sun is shining in a clear blue sky?

It is simple, clear and obvious that the world of forms are affected by the difference. When the sun shines clearly, flowers bloom, ice melts, etc.

Has the sky changed? No. Did he need to create a new sky? No. Did the clouds affect his life? Yes.

One is already the pure consciousness. You are That. You don't need to create a formless awareness capable of perceiving the beginning of the universe (how on earth could you?). Everyone is already That. Are you suffering from identification with the cloud-like thoughts? Are you suffering? Even though you may know you have within you the same consciousness as the Buddha, are you experiencing that? Does that make a difference? Would you rather not be free from suffering? When you are free from suffering at any level, do you tend to express yourself differently?

When the sun of consciousness is shining, when you are no longer identified with your body/mind/ego, it makes a difference.

When you discover you are a good guitar player, it affects the world of forms and change. Or when you improve as an architect, it affects the world of forms and change. Likewise. when you read out beautiful poetry, it affects people in a new and unique way. Why then, when you discover the treasure of treasures, do you suddenly stop becoming an affecting force in the world of forms and change?

In actuality, you don't stop affecting people; being aware has impact on others. If you have an intellectual or 'mindy' approach to life and philosophize simple truths, you will deny the existence of awakened ones and whether they can have an impact or not.

But life is mysterious and formless. It is multidimensional, with layers and layers of depth happening simultaneously. One person can meet a Buddha and just shrug their shoulders, a Buddha's wife may even shout at him! For another his mere gaze sends such waves of bliss through the devotee that sexual orgasm seems like a sneeze compared to it. Who is right? No one; the truth cannot be understood with the mind. It is all up to you.

Do you need to do something to stop identifying with your illusory ego? Yes. And at the same time you are never not the pure consciousness.

The inner path is both sudden and gradual.

If you do nothing, if you never ever hear about pure consciousness and the Buddha within, but just shoot pool, play darts, smoke cigarettes and work at a fast food joint and watch TV, you are not going to dwell in the living truth that Ramana did. But even if you do something, it doesn't mean you will either! What to do?! One must joyfully go on, dancing, seeking – some masters even talk about wishing they were ignorant again because the joy of seeking is so wonderful too.

Do you attain anything? No. But you free yourself from suffering and dwell in perpetual bliss. You are truth, consciousness, bliss. You are life.

Is there a difference between an ignorant person and a Buddha? Yes and no. No, because they are both That. Yes, because one is identified with his ego and the other isn't! Does it matter? Only you can ask yourself whether being free from suffering matters. I would suggest because forms exist, change exists, life has differences in it that it is better to be free from suffering and do something to break free from identifying with an illusory ego.

What can one do?

Do the enquiry as outlined.

Such is the nature of the beast that one must strive, but the one striving cannot reach and all striving fails. It is mysterious.

One must enquire until the enquirer disappears. Nisargadatta says, 'One must enquire ceaselessly.'

If the mystery does its thing, simply meeting a master and hearing him say 'You are That,' identifying with ego drops.

When one is ignorant, if one does nothing, nothing happens. Then one strives to attain, until eventually that very striving is the only obstacle, then the dropping of striving becomes effortless awareness. Then, one has entered into oneself and, at this point, one is sitting silently doing nothing and the grass grows by itself. One sees that one was always That and even when one looks back at the past suffering, it was never really there.

Life and the inner journey is like the Sufi story of the man who had saved up his small wages all his life to offer to a master. Upon visiting a town on his quest he hears rumor of a Sufi master who always sits by a big tree just out of town. He finds such a man and offers all his money as an offering to be taught the way. The master eyes it greedily and says to the man, 'I'll be right back,' and takes off with the bundle into town. After waiting for an hour, the man realizes he has been conned and it wasn't the master. He runs into town and frantically asks everyone if they have seen the con man. People come to help him find the thief, but he is gone. The man is distraught, his whole life's savings wasted. He heads back to the tree for one last look. He finds the master sitting there. He runs up fuming and swearing, but the master simply hands him his money back. The man cries for joy and tears of happiness stream down his face as he thanks the master for giving him his treasure back.

This awakening to oneself is intangible; you are not an object. The world of logic doesn't work here. The heart, the world of gists and sensing is closer. Although one is That, the experience of That deepens even though it is always That. How? It is unanswerable. If we are still smelling a bit of ego, we don't like the idea that someone may be deeper than us or their expression of truth is more affecting.

I have come across one Advaita master who says that enlightenment can't be the full eradication of the ego because that seems too lofty! What great logic! Enlightenment can't be this, this or this because it doesn't fit with my ideas of difficulty!

Sometimes it's good to refer to Buddha. Everyone is unique and all expressions unique, individual and at the same time one consciousness. When we dis-identify from the ego, Buddha called this liberation, and the one experiencing it he called an Arhat. We can say it is the experience of 'I am.' Buddha made a distinction between liberation and enlightenment. Liberation is when we are free from the ego in the waking state but we lose awareness during sleep. If we lose awareness during sleep, we can lose awareness during death. He called a Bodhisattva one who wishes to attain freedom in order to free others. This development of the being through loving awareness has a deeper impact on the awareness. Both are free from suffering, however, the depth of one's connection with life and the universe is mysteriously different than the one who is only concerned by his own freedom. We can say a Bodhisattva is one who unites the path of devotion with the path of awareness. He has more balls to him, more salt, more depth. He doesn't dismiss life as illusion but joyfully partakes in the sorrows of the world. His connection with others, his love of the world, his ability to fully embrace his human existence means that when he discovers the truth within, he is mysteriously more affecting in the world than the Arhat, or the one who dismisses life because it's all just an illusion.

There are many misconceptions about what a Bodhisattva is. One of them is that he gives up enlightenment to help others. This is a strange conception. Enlightenment is who you are, so how can you give up being who you are? Nirvana is how you are perceiving life; how can delaying perceiving truth be helpful?! A

Bodhisattva is one who wants to experience the truth right now! It is as though his love for the universe drives his enquiry. Eventually, like everything else, his conception of freeing others must disappear. It is said all desires turn into the one desire of finding God, but that desire too must fall away. For a Bodhisattva, the truth moves down from thinking about attaining enlightenment to help free others, to understanding the only way to help others is to free oneself and the only way to free oneself is to drop all conceptions of self and of a self helping others. The experience of enlightenment, Buddha says, is when we realize who we are before 'I am.' He says one must retain consciousness 24 hours. If we dwell in 'I am' continuously during waking state, but lose it during sleep, we may die in unconsciousness. He says, and other masters say, one must remain aware in deep sleep. One must find the witness of even the sense 'I am,' for I am is not permanent. We don't have it during deep sleep.

There are many Advaitas who are without a master and have attained the 'I am' and think that's it. That's all there is to do, because they are free from identification with thought in the waking state. While it is immense peace, the journey of joy deepens, the mystery never stops unfolding, somehow the expressions of those who have found the one truth vary even more than the ignorant who remain attached to ego.

Be wary of what you dismiss.

The ego as witness

The ego can also witness and it wants to 'attain' enlightenment. 'What a beautiful absence I have! Wow, I wonder how long I can stay in this state?' Be careful of the 'someone' who is trying to attain to the Self.

This 'someone,' when *they* are witnessing, feel they are achieving a 'state.' A difficulty for all on the path arises of splitting into two. The one who is practicing witnessing is now separate from the witness itself. It feels like the states are happening to this witness.

There are indications that the true witness has not been found and, in fact, it is still the ego who is trying to attain something. One of these is feeling that remaining in consciousness is boring. The clever ego excuse, to maintain a spiritual sense of achievement, is to use arguments such as 'one still needs to be in the world,' 'we need both wings to fly'; love and awareness, 'I'm a Zorba the Buddha.' Although these may be true in a different context, for the one who finds remaining as the witness boring, and is still subtly restless, it is not true and they are egotistical excuses.

We can use some logic. Two possibilities arise: one, that the true witness has not been found, it is merely ego witnessing, thus the true witness is not boring. Two, that remaining the witness is boring and no liberation is possible. Liberation or awakening means freedom from suffering. Being bored or restless or looking for something to happen is suffering. The witness or remaining as consciousness is another way of saying 'just being.' All the Buddhas are just being. They are not 'doing' anything, they have simply found the witness, the Self, they are pure consciousness and as such they are never bored. If being itself is boring and suffering, then no liberation or awakening is possible. We can understand clearly that when people make such statements they are trying to save their spiritual identity. It is also clear and obvious that when one is simply witnessing then there is no outside. One is never, and I mean never, bored. Whatever happens, happens. One realizes sitting alone in a room is just as inside and outside as then standing up, walking across the room, opening a door and talking to someone. Playing tennis with them, eating with them, then moving back to your room and just sitting. Nothing is affecting being. If, however, it is your ego witnessing, then there can be subtle invested interest in attaining various states of experiencing while sitting, walking, being with someone, etc. States become boring. No matter what state it is, it has to come and go, and one must maintain it. Maintaining it requires effort. Being bored suggests that the mind is looking for another, better state – that it still feels nirvana is somewhere else.

Everyone must confront and face boredom. We may chop and change our spiritual practices again and again, but at some point one has to face oneself. One has to drop all identities, all ideas that being spiritual is something better than not being spiritual. All ideas of saving the world, all ideas of being Zorba the Buddha. One must be open and innocent and in the depth of their being feel that they don't know anything. It is like a touchstone on the path towards awareness. One drops everything, even the idea of enlightenment, and stands in awe of the mystery of everything. One has to enter into the abysmal sense of losing all knowledge. One has to *know* in their blood and bones that they have never known anything. They've never known what love really is, or even if their parents are aliens! It feels like a madness, a dark night of the soul, a space where one must be prepared to drop everything. If one can go here with no expectations, then the path of inner wisdom blossoms. There is the constant feeling that one doesn't know. A wise being always hesitates to give advice; whatever they say, they know it is not right. It is the beginning of openness and freshness. The universe pulsates with a new aliveness. A tree becomes an unknowable mystery. It is such a wondrous thing. Life is so startlingly unknowable. Every living thing is seen as precious, as a throbbing beauty. Life is inexhaustibly fathomless in its mystery. One goes on and on, and the beauty and joy of being is unspeakable, depth beyond depth. It is not boring. Be wary of anyone who tells you, 'Oh, I tried the non-dual path and it's not for me.' 'Just remaining as consciousness is boring, I need to be out in the world. I'm too juicy; my path is Tantra.' These are all ideas from people who cannot be themselves. They are still restless and seeking. They are very much attached to the idea of bliss. They want another world, another state, a super juiced up non-boring state. They don't want to let go of their minds and the wonderful weave of Tantric imagination. They will say stuff like, 'I know I'm divine. I know I'm the witness,' but underneath the blissed out, juiced up, Tantric smile is a sense of looking towards something, a subtle restless discontent. That something is still needed; a special bliss is still out there.

For one who has come home to himself, all of these paths are simply mundane and ugly creations of the mind. Compared to the uncaused bliss and endless mystery of being, whatever the mind projects is simply childish.

This witness, the pure awareness is the nexus point of all seeking. No matter what path one is on, even if one is a red goddess with 18 tits and a wish-fulfilling vibrator, one has to know who they are. It is neither spiritual nor material, higher nor lower. It is simply who you are. You can't go beyond it because you will still be the witness of going beyond it. If it is eternal and timeless, it can't be caused. No matter how blissed out we may be in our Tantric identity, we know that deep down it will come to an end. It comes and goes within our awareness. Who is the one that is blissing out? Who is the one that says, 'I am a Buddha'? You are beyond even the idea of being beyond.

Being ordinary and Tantra

If you are seeking bliss, it means you don't have it. If you are projecting blissful ideas about the world and what your lifestyle should be, it means you aren't seeing the beauty of life as it is. If you are seeking bliss from others, it means you don't know yourself. The reason why that in Zen the 'ordinary' is emphasized is because life, as it is, is divine. Anything added to it is a move away from it. There is no need to listen to special music, because all music is exquisite. There is no need for special friends because all people are divine. The entire path is contained in the words 'I eat when I'm hungry, I sleep when I'm tired.' This means there is no experience other than what is happening sought in his mind. There is no state he is seeking other than the one he is in. Why? Because life is perfect as it is. Tantra is an intermediary technique to get to this place of no place.

People on this earth at this current moment are, in general, miserable. In the last city I lived in, I came across, at the most, five happy people. I am being generous too. Out of thousands of people I witnessed, maybe one a month had an aura of contentment or a radiance to them. Outdated religions and concepts, and a society still modeled on them are crippling people's natural state of joy. Tantra is a helpful way for people to change their conceptual and emotional framework. The preposterous notion that life is a sin and being alive is fundamentally wrong has been perpetuated for millennia by religions. It has gone deep. Tantra is a conscious effort to make aware to people that life is bliss. Life is fun, joyful, playfulness. The deepest wound on humans by religion is that the natural energy moving through us that they label 'sex' is condemned. Thus, Tantra is heavily linked with sex because it is such an obvious and natural state of bliss. It is also the most condemned and polluted with seriousness. Mythological images are used to ignite inside of us a sense of our natural being, which is beauty and bliss. Still, to this day, it is considered a crime to acknowledge that we are God. Happiness is still considered weird. Tantra is a way to bring out the radiance. It is effort and technique. It is conscious effort to be divine. When one is playing with Krishna like Papaji did, or one is viewing themselves as a goddess or daka, and life is great fun, then one has to drop all of that and look within at who it is that is divine. One has to find the uncaused one. The one that, without effort, is bliss. When this is found, the world is beyond any imagined idea about it. One sees that everyone is a Buddha. There is nowhere to go. Nothing to achieve. No desire to be anything else. One *is*.

So, one has to be careful one isn't practicing Tantra as an excuse to avoid sitting with one's being as a cover-up for one's attachments and addictions. It is important to step out on the journey in the correct way. If we have wrong reasons, we will find it difficult to just be. Maybe it is to fit in better socially, maybe we want to be subtly more powerful than others, so we can walk in a room and others will notice our subtle special aura. Maybe we got interested for reasons of the occult because we met a master and he always seemed in control and powerful. Maybe we wanted to escape from society and get really blissed out. Maybe we couldn't deal with our anger problem and we want rid of anger. Maybe we are really identified with who we think we are and we want as much pleasure as possible, and Tantra seems the best way to get it. Whatever way, and wherever we are in our life, it is important to know that one is already that. That our natural being is effortless, free, bliss, non-suffering. It is not something to be practiced or created. It is already the case. It is our very consciousness. Although this may be intellectual at first, it is important to know it. We don't have to hold on to these kinds of indicators continuously; we can check in every now and again. Am I making effort? Am I free from suffering? Am I simply bliss with no desire? If not, then we can accept, keep quiet and happy, and stay on the path. It is a joyful path in itself.

If we've tried 'just being' and found it 'boring' and want some Tantric excitement then know, quietly and simply, you never found your true being. Enjoy your Tantric practice, have fun, but be wary of disparaging and disdaining. The true being with no identity has not been found yet. If one finds 'the practice' of 'I am' (it is not practice, although it may seem like that to the mind) boring, it means wrong identification is still there. This can help with the path of awareness. Being aware there is something beyond this, being aware that perhaps one is fooling oneself, that one still hasn't passed the boredom phase one has to go through. Be aware that one is still an ego and is seeking excitement and 'hits' and is looking for another thing to try. Traditionally, Tantra was taught secretly because it is so easy to deceive oneself and fall back into chasing desire. Feeling that happiness is a state to achieve and getting addicted to experiences and missing the point of coming home to pure awareness. One was first given the task of breaking free from strong physical identifications. These days, people get upset if they have to share! They may have incredible material possessions, such as warm houses all through the year, running hot water, cars – abundance upon abundance – but simply just sharing some of it without something in return burns their emotions. This is once again the hungry spirit realm talked about by Buddha, the state of consciousness where you have your cake and want to eat it. You have and have but don't find the happiness you seek and yet can't abide the idea of simply giving your food, or time, to someone else. A businessman's mindset is there, all in new age language to maintain a spiritual ego identity. 'Don't give your power away.' 'Don't just give something to someone; make sure it is an equal energy exchange.' This needy mindset is well below an animal's consciousness and awareness. Spiritual practices can help make people more human, kind and loving; they may be cultivated. Due to the insanity of such things as Christianity upon the psyche, some alternative mindset and effort can be needed.

To help people from not making the mistake of making Tantra a part of their neediness or it becoming a double-edged sword, and instead of helping someone break free from identity, it binds them tighter to chasing bliss, resulting in licentiousness and jealousy and selfishness. Small doses of sexual transformation were introduced; the trick is to always fall back into the heart practice of self-awareness. One immediately falls into the place of no place. Thus, one can use everything to help in our self-awareness. But the true way is to begin from self-awareness. Everything must come back to self-awareness. One must feel free to express their humanity with freedom and joy; the point is we are deeply identified with the body and mind. If we start chasing bliss, it may well deepen the attachment to the human expression and, in the end, keep one bound to suffering. If one finds the Self, the witness, true being, then life happens spontaneously and it is pure joy. To find this, one doesn't have to deny any part of life. It can be a tricky business. Thus, the master can be a great help.

Nations and old identities are out of date

There is a deep need of the ego or the 'person' to have a sense of control. This need pervades the material and spiritual world. We want to figure out life. This is quite clear in the physical world. Science has led us to an abundance of comfort. Unfortunately, control and fear are walking hand in hand and the mind that forged its way to physical comforts has yet to cease. The mind that wants to be free from danger and have enough food. The mind that is afraid of strange lands. The mind that thinks the world is an infinite resource. The mind that thinks we have to work and fight our way through life to keep ourselves sustainable. This mind is no longer relevant. It is no longer contextual.

We are now a one-world culture. We are; it has happened. People may still fight and deny it. It is, however, so clearly stupid to maintain the old national identities. I live in Scotland and people are fiercely proud to be Scottish. However, if you look at it openly, it is absurd. What is it about them that is Scottish? Their body? Our bodies are made and sustained by the food we eat. Almost none of it comes from Scotland. Our food is produced from around the world. The clothes they wear are not all from Scotland. Can the air be called Scottish? It is patently absurd. The language they speak is English; the thoughts in their minds are in English. The education they receive is from ideas from people all around the world. Their entertainments are mainly from United States, or other countries. What is it you can point to about them that is 'Scottish'? The slight variation in the tone of their voice? This analysis can be applied to almost every country. If we have even slight wisdom, what I am saying is obvious. The people living before Columbus arrived on the patch of land we at present time communally call United States, thought the idea of owning land was absurd. It was so stupid they couldn't even conceive of the idea. We know intellectually, very easily, they are just ideas. But intellect is one thing, lived experience another. I've met seekers who got upset because their president was made fun of!

But ideas believed in are, if we really check, the only real danger. We are at such a beautiful point in time where we can drop old ideas of nationality because it doesn't take much of a Zen whack on the head to clear them out of the mind. If you go to London, to say it is an 'English' city is simply preposterous! Of course, things are slightly different from other cities, such as the color of the buses and the quality of food, but that's about it. Is that worth keeping the old identities for? Worth fighting over? The people in Ireland fought for decades, but for what? Was it food, water, the ability to sustain life, shelter? Was it not just so they could say that, 'This is Ireland'?

But our identities are everything to us, even though they are nothing.

We are a one-world culture. The Internet is a one-world voice. We are watching the same shows all around the world. We are receiving our information from all around the world. I can be in South Africa quicker, by flying, than the other end of my country if I travel by bus! I interact with people from all over the world every day, physically too. My food is from all over the world. The spiritual books from all over the world are now freely available. In this light, the old school religions look as stupid as people identifying with their old nationalities.

Can't we embrace this new culture? Can't we create a new way?

If we fully embrace a one-world identity now, how long will it be before the future generations cannot even conceive of an idea of fighting among themselves? We are told from history books that cultures with a deeper and truer lifestyle that embraced life and had a more non-dualistic outlook on life have lived in peace. It is possible. How long before the coming generations have a mind that realizes this world is not an inexhaustible resource and wants to live in a more sustainable, harmonious way?

We could easily live, like cultures of old, with minimal amount of work for anyone and the rest of the time could be for play, joy, inner exploration and a profound love for life and oneself.

We know from our own experience it is difficult to give up old identities. People often don't want to go without a fight. However, everything is already in place. We need a one-world government, a one-world flag, a one-world identity. The old identities will persist for a while but, as we know, as is just said, we already are a one-world culture.

Identity can feel as close to us as our own breathing. We don't even know that we have it. Hence the help from a master. It can be difficult to observe our own world neutrally and honestly. Even great and accomplished musicians and actors work with others to gain a more truthful and helpful perspective. Of course, ultimately no one can help and one must speak from one's own authority. The American Indian example is a good indication of how deep conditioning and identification can be. It took them years to even process the idea that a human being born into this world, living on it for a few years and then disappearing out of it, could own it. Once they understood the concept, they couldn't believe how stupid it was! Now, for the people living on that land, that concept is probably a bigger concept and sense of who they are than their own bodies. Yet, it is preposterous and non-existent in terms of reality. For people, it just seems like owning their land is a truth so self-evident, no one even thinks about it. Very quickly, from not existing in the minds of the people, it has become as if it is the very mind itself. Powerful identification is sustained by a lifestyle reinforcing it. Hence the truth needs to be told again and again. Repeated again and again. One never knows when the identity will pop and one will see that it is not the truth. The awakened one understands these are simply concepts believed in. They also understand that the belief causes untold suffering.

It is a strange state of affairs to witness another human being, so unique, so beautiful, so extraordinary, so alive, born into a paradise of wonder, so full of treasures, wonders unexplored, creativity and natural love, suffering for nothing. Just an idea believed in. To witness this concept crush his soul into anguish, when you can see their inner light but they can't. When you know they won't understand when you say 'life is bliss.' How can they?

The identification is like a limpet on their heart. The Buddhas, with eyes of compassion, devise ways and means to pop the identity.

Be wary of people who say, 'You don't need a master' and 'You don't need to do anything, we're already all enlightened.' Who do so with a subtle fragrance of arrogance. Who, like the person working on a crossword puzzle, suddenly gets it and says, 'Oh, that's so obvious' and then proceeds to laugh at people because they don't get how obvious it is.

Be wary of people who claim to know the truth but can't seem to recognize untruth, the people who are suffering and not seeing it.

Actually, have some fun with them and tell them to go to the heart of the Bible Belt in America and tell them that Christianity is just a concept. Go to their gun rallies and tell them there is no such thing as 'America' and their identification is causing them suffering, and see what happens.

Clearly identification has depth, hence awakening is both gradual and instant. Seekers of old after decades of effort would then hear a few words from the master, when they were ready to hear words such as 'drop all effort' and 'you are already that' and they would 'pop.' The master wouldn't go to a neo-Nazi rally and say, 'There is no such thing as black or white.'

I feel it is good to be aware of all levels at once. Ultimately, we understand we are already what we seek. This is our heart practice, although, of course, it is not even a practice. We, however, never deny life. We must accept where we are at and the multiplicity of our life and all its subtle identifications. People want to skip ahead because they have an intellectual understanding of the teachings. Remember identifications can be so powerful that they too *feel* true. If someone is Scottish and you make fun of Scotland they *feel* insulted even though, in reality, there is no such thing as Scotland, but it *feels* real. So much so, people will hate you for it, they will forge their identity with you based on what you say about the concept rattling around in their head, about their idea of what a country is. This is just a country! The journey is to break identification with your very idea of who you think you are! The work is breaking through the untrue. Nothing needs to be done to create awakening or a new consciousness. How can you possibly create consciousness?! How can the ego create consciousness?! It is just like the concept that a human being can own the land. The consciousness is there, an ego arises out of it, feels it owns consciousness, then disappears back into consciousness.

The identification is like our blood and bones, but with true understanding it can 'pop' just like getting a crossword puzzle. It is that sense of suddenly getting it, but the suddenly getting it is not out with the work on it. We must never forget it can happen any time, because you are already consciousness, you are here, you are life.

An indicator we have popped is we have no desire, we are content, we live in a quiet constant bliss. We are no longer looking outside of what is happening for another experience to replace it.

Identification can be subtle. Even someone as enlightened as Gangaji appeared to get caught up in it recently. Her husband had an affair and, according to the reports, there was a subtle condemnation towards him that he had done wrong and that he would learn. This is just Christian conditioning. There is nothing wrong with falling in love. There is nothing wrong with having sex. Nothing. It is just our conditioning that makes us *feel* it is wrong. It is not. If we are truly not identifying, then some noise may come into the mind about this and that from our conditioning about sexuality, but one simply observes it. Conditioning doesn't just go away like that, the mind still has a momentum, the freedom is in being undisturbed. There is nothing for or against the mind. If one is actually really ruffled by their partner being free to put their body parts next to someone else, or, have an emotional connection with another human being. If one is really upset and feels it to be wrong, but tries to say they are just witnessing it all, are they really an unidentified observer? Are they truly free from concepts? This is where it gets very subtle and difficult to talk about in words. There is nothing wrong with anger arising, there is no judgment for or against. But has that anger arisen on the winds of conditioning and is it merely observed, or, is their identification with a self that *feels* the moral codes one was taught as a child are true? Does the anger arise because one feels one is right and the other is wrong, and one *tries* to witness to maintain a subtle spiritual identity?

Workshop enlightenment

In our fast spiritual food culture, we have our McDonald's sannyasins who, more often than not, consider themselves 'Big Macs.' They smack of spiritual arrogance, dismissing all paths because Osho did, looking down on others because they have an intellectual grasp of enlightenment. They attend a weekend enlightenment retreat, experience some release of their emotional tensions and think they are free. One of the dangers of the McDonald's sannyasins is that they become addicted to workshops. It is an age-old phenomenon of feeling the release of tensions as spiritual awakening. Moving between one extreme to another is blissful; they presume this bliss is what the mystics refer to as 'satchitananda.' Unfortunately, these morons are too proud to ever follow a master for if they do, they never fully give their heart over; they keep one subtle layer over their hearts. Sometimes it takes a few years but eventually they talk about the master in dismissive terms and, because they can't face their spiritual failure, they take this subtle anger as independence and self-awareness and wisdom. But they never fully committed. There was deep down an ulterior motive and fear of losing the ego and being truly vulnerable.

This is why workshops are dangerous. They are contrived and sterile environments for those who are so afraid to be vulnerable, they need a super extra crutch just to get them on their feet. Thus, they need a controlled environment. One does not need to *trust*, because in a workshop it is a managed space with like-minded people. Like all medicines it can be very helpful in the beginning, and it can give a seeker a transitional flavor of a better way of being and feeling. However, if one lacks trust, one will become addicted to workshops and being in that environment. Control freaks are drawn to them because everything is always managed, and there are distinct boundaries. Be wary of anyone claiming to be a Tantric master who is addicted to workshops or has had their training and awakenings through workshops, whose only commitment was for two weeks at a time. The only real commitment is lifelong. Anyone can go somewhere and feel good about themselves for a couple of weeks. The real work begins when you know there is no going back.

Tantra is trust in life. If one has never trusted, going through the way of workshops can be helpful to get you out there in life, living as one always wanted. When one starts speaking from the heart in life. It will happen in dangerous places. It may risk one's job and income, or social group, or it will make you look like a total idiot with no hope of changing that image. When one is doing it, not to even be Tantric but because it is the only way one can be, then one is moving on the path of Tantra and awakening.

Trusting in life is singing for no reason in a public space, on your own, because that was what felt right. Being yourself in the wild, wild world is where the real Tantra and trust starts. If you can't do this, you will levitate towards trying different and new sparkly workshops, where you are in control and everything is safe. You will deceive yourself because you may be cathartic or trying something 'new,' but the environment is fake.

Remember, trust has nothing to do with outcomes. You may start singing in a bar and get a good beating, but only one who trusts knows its value; it can't be explained.

Workshop people, the spiritual Burger Kings, in essence, just want to hang out with people like them and have similar experiences with like-minded people. This, of course, is very immature and retarded, but we have to start somewhere. We need to eventually become adults and express ourselves in the world where everyone is different and no one has the same outlook as you. One of the aspects that makes us adult is when we realize everyone is different from us.

A: I am in a relationship but I have fallen in love with someone else.

Chobo: This can be problematic if we are dominated by our feelings. As with thoughts, if the emotional center is the master and not the servant, we find ourselves at the whims of feelings. Do feelings simply control your life and are you happy with this situation?

Love, for most people, is mixed with possession, which causes pain. Also when you engage sexually with another being, your energy continuum changes with your current partner; polygamy has to accept those consequences. It is important to check deep down that you are not reveling in the drama, and enjoying the excitement of your life being messed up? And you may find this commotion and emotional turmoil is how you identify yourself. It is what gives you happiness. What *you* feel happiness to be. It is difficult to transcend something if you don't actually want to! But, if you can recognize, deeply and honestly, where you are, it is a beautiful space for self-awareness to flow into your life.

The experiences you are having may be great but the experience must lead to transcendence or you will just keep going like this. You have to be able to see through it, to be tired of it, the drama. To see that it isn't actually fulfilling but is distracting from your true center. If you lean towards the Sufi way, then you must focus your inner light on the center of the spinning wheel of emotional life and find the still place that never changes. Thus using the experience for transcendence. If you are still clinging to wild experiences you will miss, it is delicate... the words: center and truth, can sound cold; what I mean is: you are love. If you are 'finding' love then it will disappear too, if you are having an experience it will end, when you realize you are love, then you are love. The wildness is a distraction from reality. Our lives are a sloppy paint job over nirvana, the experience of who we are stripped naked of the other.

A: What should I do? Is there a practice to help? I like falling in love though.

C: Spiritual practices can be another attempt at control. Transcendence doesn't mean not having or giving up; it means no more relevance. You don't transcend chairs, because they are not an issue. The experiences you are having indicate a space within you untouched by them, beyond them, pure and who you really are. When you experience the revelation that your 'being' is love, then you are content to be alone. When you are content with your being then you can love your partner in ways you never dreamed of.

We can say we have four levels going deeper and deeper from the physical, to mental, to emotional, to being. Just as a deep emotional life is incomparable to just a heady life, so a life at the level of being is incomparable to being emotional. And in the same way that being emotional doesn't mean you can't think, so resting in your being doesn't mean you can't be emotional. This requires surrender. I would say for the time being just ask yourself: Am I more than my emotions? And get back to me. And ask it very innocently and deeply without looking for any ready-made answer.

A: But I know this already!

C: Intellectually everyone thinks they are more; experientially I've met very few in this lifetime.

A: I know I'm the divine.

C: I don't believe you. Your life is pointing out to you that you are not resting in your being. Your emotional pain, and itchy desires, indicate an intellectual understanding of the truth and reveal you are still identified with personal self. I can't give you any personal advice to help deal with your emotions; for one, I don't know; and two, it would be undignified, so, if you really feel out the question i.e. feel it rather than ask it with internal words, the arising experience will be more helpful. If you are more than your emotions who are you?

A: The self.

C: When your emotions want something new can you rest in the Self? Do you always have to have what you desire? Are you at some point going to move beyond the whims of desire? If you are the divine surely that is where you would rather be?

Before I go, I would say again that you don't want to give up the pain. Nirvana is here and now, right now! The fact you are not experiencing it means there is still strong identification with the ego pain and it is scared of just being. Find out what you REALLY want first.

I'm not, therefore I am

There is a strange phenomenon in the Advaita community. Many people I have spoken to seem to think everything exists except people! It is odd. They happily accept you can see a chair, or anger exists, but there is no such thing as a person! This is an extreme position.

We have to exist to be able to refute our non-existence!

I want to make clear the difference between non-existence and the true self.

If you are alone in your room right now (or just imagine) turn to your right and start talking to the empty space next to you. Is it male or female? Is it tall or short? Is it human? Speak to it. Is it even an it? Is it even formless? Or is it simply there is nothing there? This is non-existence. Clearly this is not the same as meeting someone.

It is not a question of do we exist or not, but what is the nature of our existence.

A person exists, but only as an appearance to our mind's eye. The suffering arises when we feel the person is more than the thought and appearance. The person who is more than a thought and appearance does not exist at all.

It is like this: You turn round again and imagine next to you a pink unicorn. There is no pink unicorn existing outside of your imagination. No one else can see your private projection. However, it does exist as a private projection. That's fine, lovely, you can sing a song about how pink the unicorn you are picturing is! There is no problem when you understand the correct nature of the appearance. What if, however, you start investing all your energy into your pink unicorn, and in fact start talking to it, as if it were *more real* than it is? Imagine others bought into it and started asking you how your unicorn is today. Imagine this went on from the time you were born until forty years had passed.

Imagine you had made a career on your 'conversations with my pink unicorn.' Now, someone awake finds you in this position. He will say to you: '*That* unicorn, the one you have made extra real, doesn't exist. It doesn't exist. An imagined unicorn does.' However, forty years of continual belief creates a strong habit and for a while when the pink unicorn appears you still feel it's real; you forget again that it is just a created projection.

The purpose of Satsang and meditation, of understanding the truth and sitting silently, is recognizing the personal self is not the true self. Once recognized, sitting silently allows the space to grow between 'being' and the projection. It deepens the impact of the truth. Engaging solely in activities is a more difficult way. It is not that meditation is a special 'thing' in and of itself. It is simply that we have cultivated an ego through our engagement with others. Many of our problems merely arise through habit. Mind resuscitates itself through unconscious habit. If we have a glimpse of truth, and then throw ourselves back into all our old habits, the 'I' that we have always identified with arises immediately and we believe in it. It is very helpful to sit without doing anything, because there is no need to have any sense of a practical person. It is easier, for most people, to sit, in order to find the inner space which witnesses the personal 'I.'

When we have a body and mind there arises in us an appearance of a person. Whatever we change in the body and mind will change the appearance of the personal I arising. It is an ever-changing personal identification. It is quite natural. If we cut our hair off we have a different 'I' appearing to our mind's eye, or cut our leg off we will have a different appearing phenomenal self-image. Great. The suffering comes because we think that appearing self-image is who we are. It is not. This self does not exist on its own outside of *our* seeing its appearance. It does exist *as* an appearance. What is the *our* that sees a picture, an appearance of 'I'? This is the uncaused, unchanging presence, the awareness that witnesses everything happening in the universe. It is formless, so, like the empty space next to you I asked you to talk to, it cannot be seen with the eyes or senses. However, unlike the space of non-existence where there is nothing, this formless presence is the foundation of the universe. It is exists but not as a thing. Everything that has ever happened has existed within the realm of awareness. This is a far cry from someone saying, 'You don't exist.'

It is simply that you don't exist the way you think you exist at the moment. When you realize that the appearing 'I' is not you, cannot be you because it is appearing to you, you will understand that it is *not* who you are. When you can see I am not that, I am not this, what is left is a non-phenomenal being, a state of am-ness. Thus, I am not (what I was previously relating to) therefore I am (what has always been here).

Everything is not just consciousness

We cannot say, 'It's all just consciousness.' Another human being is not my consciousness, or a boat is not my consciousness. You cannot pick up a jacket and say, 'This jacket is my consciousness.' Neither can you say it is separate from consciousness. The world is both consciousness and external at the same time. This is the mystery.

The mystery is appearing to consciousness. When we understand everything is appearing we understand nothing is separate. We also understand that things ARE appearing. We don't deny appearance, nor condemn it, as if the unknowable and wonderful universe appearing before us is worthless. The appearances are consciousness coloring in existence, a mysterious divine artwork. The illusion is when we take our own private appearances to be the actual way things are.

When we think everything is just consciousness, we feel we are the center of the universe. That life is just a dream. Life is dream LIKE. This was a technique to help seekers understand that like a dream the world does not exist separately from your consciousness. But a dream is still just a private appearance. Private appearance is the important term. That is why someone is said to awaken from the sleep of ignorance. He no longer exists in a private dreamworld i.e. you no longer feel the private appearances you are having are the way things are.

So, life, LIFE! Is not 'all just an illusion'! This attitude has caused so many problems. Life is vast, we are a small stream in the great ocean of life, but, we are not separate either!

Objects are phenomenal; awareness is non-phenomenal. But they exist together. Buddha said, 'form is empty; emptiness is form.' When mystics talk about the 'play of existence,' they are using the idea that objects help awareness to find itself. It is like the invisible man! If the invisible man was loose in a deaf and anosmia commune how would he be found? They would have to throw a tub of paint on him. The paint would give him his form to enable communication. The image forming from the paint would not be his form, but neither would it be separate from his form. If one of the deaf, anosmia people was also color-blind (roll with it) and saw the paint as red, he would have an appearance of a private red invisible man. While the man who has 'normal' vision would see a green man.

This is like objects and consciousness. A splatter of body parts and thoughts has been thrown over the formless consciousness, in order for it to perceive itself?! Who knows, can anyone really say why life is?

While seeking, awareness is given greater importance because we are not in tune with ourselves. Once in accord, the world falls into its proper (i.e. harmonious) place. Also, the world cannot be taken with us when we die. How do we know this? Because it is already the case! We no longer have the same body we had as a child, we have a different mind, we have a different person we call 'I,' our house is decaying, everything is dead in comparison to how it was. The awareness has not changed.

The middle way is the perpetual ability to balance the ever-changing processes of life. The one on the middle way will always be different, because he is spontaneously responsive. On a personal level, we begin by being entrenched in the external appearances; to bring us out, a master may tell us they don't exist, may make us abandon them for a time being completely. Because of this, we may move to the other extreme, and feel the 'world' is useless, not real, an illusion, you don't exist so nothing matters. When this is seen as an extreme, we will love, honor and joyfully play out our human existence while dwelling as awareness or being. We will truly be called a human being when we are fully in the world and fully free within. We will then easily embrace all the myriad differences while maintaining an under-lying unity with all beings. This is how everyone can be. This is the paradise on earth. All it is, is understanding oneself. Understanding oneself is the greatest gift you can give to others. May everyone delve deep within and be a selfish bodhisattva.

In this mesmeric flow of everything
Someone falls in front of me and I watch as I catch
This meeting with, at my best guess, I call a human being
Is so perpetually unique, I again flower anew in formless
    depth
Oh sweet mystery
You dance over to me again
The feeling I felt when I was forgiven
Lifted me beyond my self to the magic realm of acceptance
Where no one surrendered to nothing
In the greatest illusory show called life
Where nothing was figured out and nothing changed
But My God how we danced, oh, how we dance...

BOOKS

O is a symbol of the world, of oneness and unity. In different cultures it also means the "eye," symbolizing knowledge and insight. We aim to publish books that are accessible, constructive and that challenge accepted opinion, both that of academia and the "moral majority."

Our books are available in all good English language bookstores worldwide. If you don't see the book on the shelves ask the bookstore to order it for you, quoting the ISBN number and title. Alternatively you can order online (all major online retail sites carry our titles) or contact the distributor in the relevant country, listed on the copyright page.

See our website **www.o-books.net** for a full list of over 500 titles, growing by 100 a year.

And tune in to myspiritradio.com for our book review radio show, hosted by June-Elleni Laine, where you can listen to the authors discussing their books.

mySpiritRadio